LIFE WHIMSY

How to Think, Play, and Work More Creatively

Published 2023

Book Design by Natalie McGuire Design
Photography by Abby Grace Photography *(unless noted otherwise)*

Printed in the United States of America
First Edition

ISBN 979-8-9873372-0-2

*For my dad, who told me
I could be anything
I wanted to be.*

I STILL BELIEVE YOU.

Life Whimsy

HOW TO THINK, PLAY, AND WORK MORE CREATIVELY

Table of Contents

Introduction

I learned how to upholster chairs back in 2012 as a way to express my creativity, to have a new hobby, and to have some fun. I had no idea this adventure would change my life, sparking a career change, and setting me on a road to help other women.

But for me, it's not just about the chairs.

My passion is creativity.

In my 50+ years, creativity has been the key to everything that brings me joy. It has been my medication during seasons of burnout. It is the key ingredient for daily happiness. And it has brought me satisfaction through my work. So many of us just don't know how to tap into our creativity because we've been distracted by technology, felt too uninspired to try, or experienced hardships that have sucked the life out of us. Consciously or unconsciously, many of us have abandoned our creative natures.

When I was a little girl, I set my stuffed animals in front of my chalkboard like good little students and taught them from my stack of teacher-edition books. I didn't realize it then, but looking back, I can see that teaching was in my DNA. It wasn't until I was in my mid-20s that I realized I should go back to school and get my teaching degree. I taught 3rd, 5th, and 7th grades, and the classroom became a unique place to express my creativity. After getting my master's degree in gifted education, I realized I loved creating curriculum. That personal "lightbulb moment" shouldn't have been a surprise either, because in the classroom, I was always creating fun ways for my students to learn the grade-level content. The love of curriculum writing set me off to a new career as a writer and presenter for a small publishing company for many years. It was there that I was able to channel my creativity through my writing.

In the meantime, I am always pushing myself outside of my work to do things to make me more creative. Putting myself in uncomfortable situations to learn new things helps me grow as an individual. My risk-taking nature helps me to think more creatively. If I can think more creatively, then I can produce more creative work. One of these "risks" I took was learning how to revamp chairs. I spent five Saturdays in a shop down in South Austin learning the ins and outs of the skill of upholstery. Then I spent six more weeks honing my skills in another class. This undertaking was fun, frustrating, head-ache producing, and exhilarating all at the same time.

Designing chairs is just one of the many ways I express my creativity. My home overflows with my creative projects and makeovers. My environment is my palette where I show how I think about design and try out new ideas. And I'm having a lot of fun in the process. Being a business owner gives me an additional outlet to explore my creativity in venues such as marketing my products and teaching my online classes. For me, the challenges never end because there's always a problem to solve and something new to create.

I wrote this book for those of you
who desire to live more creatively
in how you think, play, and work.

*I have organized my book
into three main parts to help you
in your journey.*

HOW TO THINK MORE CREATIVELY: For years, I've taken my creative thinking for granted, not realizing how this thinking was impacted by my positive psychology practices, strategies to wrangle my fears, and brainstorming and visualizing multiple options. These techniques have made me a more creative thinker. In this book, I'm sharing my strategies, processes, and thoughts in hopes that these will help you to develop your creative thinking strategies.

HOW TO PLAY MORE CREATIVELY: I show the ways I play, have fun, and enjoy life. So many adults have forgotten to take time to play. In fact, many adults don't even know how to play anymore. Playing is important because it's what rejuvenates our creativity and keeps burnout at bay. My hope is that by sharing the ways I play, it will spark some ideas for you to spend more time playing in ways *you* enjoy, too.

HOW TO WORK MORE CREATIVELY: Finally, work doesn't have to be just work. We can infuse creativity into our jobs whether we work a mainstream job or are an artisan by trade. I have to be creative to make a living. But many of us work nine-to-five jobs where creativity may not be *required* of us. That work context doesn't mean you abandon your spark; you can bring creativity into any job. In this book, I show various motivators to help get us through any boring or not-so- glamorous work that has to be done. I hope my business journey from a side hustle to growing it to my full time job inspires you to do the same if that's your desire. By sharing the lessons I've learned along the way, my hope is that your journey to a creative business will be stimulating and successful.

Enjoy your journey!

xo,
Wendy

PART I:

Unlock
your
creative
thinking

Here's to the crazy ones. The misfits. The rebels. The troublemakers. The round pegs in the square holes. The ones who see things differently...
—Rob Siltanen

Design ideas pop into my head all the time. I decide to add a new chair to a room to bring in more whimsy, or I think of a new use for a unique accessory. Sometimes my design ideas are about introducing a new color into a space. These ideas come both naturally and unexpectedly to me. It is the result of how I've trained myself to think more creatively.

Creativity is not something magical or something with which only certain people are born. An enormous lie people tell themselves is that they are not creative and never will be. The truth is, creativity is something you can develop over time. There is no age limit on creativity—you don't reach a certain age and use it up. In fact, the opposite can be quite true; you can become *more* creative as you age.

Creativity all begins with how you think—to be a more creative person, you must be a creative thinker. This kind of thinking can be learned, which is good news for anyone who wants to think of themselves as a creative person. It doesn't matter if you've been told in the past that you are not creative. Regardless of where you are on the creativity scale, you can start developing or building your creativity right now.

CHAPTER 1:

Your Permission Slip

to be

Creative

Wouldn't it be fun to have the best ideas in the room, to have people look *to you* for inspiration, and in the meantime, get the most out of living your life? It's possible. But you have to nurture your own creativity first.

Everyone has the potential to be more creative. Our creativity grows when we try new things because it opens us up to new experiences and ways of thinking. Sometimes new thinking is uncomfortable, and we get stretched in the process. But when we put ourselves in situations where we can flex those creative muscles, we carve out opportunities for creativity to happen. The more you practice your creativity, the more creative you will become.

However, there are roadblocks that hold us back from becoming more creative. Most of these hindrances are a result of our mindset.

WE GIVE ALL KINDS OF EXCUSES FOR NOT LIVING UP TO OUR POTENTIAL CREATIVE SELVES:

I'm too old; I'm afraid I have nothing left to offer.

I'm too young; I don't have enough experience.

I've got kids; it's not my turn yet.

I've got too many bills; I don't have enough money.

I'm too busy; I don't have time to enjoy things.

I don't believe I can be creative; I'm scared I'll find out for sure that I'm not.

What is your excuse?

Jane, who is now seventy-six, had a long career in the corporate world. But at age seventy-two, she decided to try upholstery. She loved it so much that she started a chair business. Each month, she stages her gorgeous chairs at an artisan market alongside framed art, floral arrangements, and painted furniture. She also takes custom orders and ships all over the country. Jane's age hasn't stopped her from trying new things.

Lindsay Ekstrom, a young Dallas-based artist and mother, paints cultural icons dressed in pop culture clothing—picture George Washington wearing a blue Gucci suit. Just a little over four years ago, she picked up a set of oil paints at a thrift store and taught herself how to paint portraits by watching YouTube videos. Today, she exhibits at an art gallery, sells prints, and paints commissions that demand premium prices. She didn't let her lack of formal training or her youth stop her from trying something new.

The excuses we give for not living up to our potential creative selves are not imagined. We have real responsibilities and are being pulled in many directions, which can drain away our creativity. This stress leads to us just going through the motions of life, fulfilling our duties to everyone else while neglecting the very thing that gives us the joy of living... our creativity.

But we don't have to choose between "being responsible" and nurturing our creativity. We can do both.

It begins with giving ourselves permission.

Listen
to your
inner
desires

You Have my Permission

It may sound silly that a grown woman has to give herself permission to do anything. But most women tend to put everyone else first; it's what we've been taught to do. We want to do right by our families, friends, and society, so we tell ourselves we can't want things for ourselves.

The truth is that we are not doing our family any favors by putting ourselves last; it's a bad example for our kids—do we really want them doing the same? They will follow our lead. I'm not saying to only think of ourselves to the detriment of our families. I'm just arguing that we need to put ourselves on equal footing with everyone else. There should be a healthy dose of "yes" at times.

It's a big step to start listening to our inner desires and acting upon them. But when we give ourselves permission to live more creatively, the payoff is huge. So how do we begin to give ourselves permission when we have been taught to do the opposite of that our whole life?

PERMISSION TO EMBRACE YOUR OWN DREAMS

We can begin by allowing ourselves to embrace our dreams. Embrace your own dreams—not just the dreams for your loved ones and kids, but your *own* dreams. You are allowed to have your own dreams. Do you even know what those dreams are? Take some time, and let yourself dream big. When we cut loose the tethers of everyone else's dreams, we can begin to expand what we hope for in our own future. What are your dreams?

PERMISSION TO ADMIT
TO THE THINGS YOU LOVE

What do you really love? The color orange? Christmas ornaments? Suede shoes? Get in touch with your inner desires, listen to your gut, and act on it. Decorate the way you want, wear what you want, and design what you want. Figure out what you like, and admit it to the world by acting upon it. This mindset is liberating for us and inspiring to others when we finally start living our best lives.

PERMISSION TO CARVE OUT TIME FOR YOURSELF

Carve out time for the things you want to do. You will often figure out what you want through playing; yes, playing. You might not grab the nearest swing, but take time for yourself to explore new ideas; try new things; and indulge in activities that you really love doing or might just want to try. Tell yourself it's okay to goof off, read a book, take a walk, or go window shopping. The important thing is to take the time off from your other duties to just be with yourself, absorbing the world around you and doing what you want to do.

Both Jane and Lindsay didn't start their creative explorations with the goal of creating businesses or finding success. They just decided to try something new for the pure joy of creating. Jane was looking to expand her knowledge and design her own chairs. Lindsay needed something tactile to do so she could pull herself out of her postpartum depression after the birth of her third child. These women found joy first and foremost, and it began by giving themselves permission to explore creatively.

Giving ourselves time to think and play is how we nurture our creativity. The payoff to our well-being is well worth it and not a waste of time.

Creativity improves our quality of life,
provides excitement, and gives us
the joy of coming up with great ideas.

CONCLUSION

Sometimes all we need is a permission slip. I'm giving you permission to be creative—to bring more whimsy into your life. Not everything we do will turn out successful or profitable... it's not about that. It's about the journey of creating. We often surprise ourselves when we go into creative endeavors with no expectations but just looking to experience something new, play around, have some fun, and try something. Make *today* the day you begin your creative journey by giving yourself permission to do so.

Permission Slip

I GIVE MYSELF PERMISSION TO:

_____

_____

_____

_____

_____

SIGNED: _____

CHAPTER 2:
Crafting Creative
Ideations

Photo by Hector M Sanchez Photography

everal years ago for Mother's Day, my oldest daughter painted me a Frida Kahlo portrait. I found an old frame from the local antique mall and hung it on my stairwell wall. Over the next several holidays, she painted more Frida portraits to add to my collection until there were six of them. During the fall of 2018, I had an idea to use these six Frida paintings on a set of chairs. I took pictures of the paintings and sent them off to be printed on fabric. Then, I began to brainstorm ideas for color schemes. I remember telling a friend that this idea was either ridiculous or genius. I'm not sure either of those was accurate, but it was original and unique for chairs at that time.

When I collaborated with Carrie Schmitt to use her art on my chairs, I gathered coordinating fabrics and found a quiet space in my home to brainstorm ideas for this new collection of chairs. First, I laid out her fabrics all over my furniture so I could see each one clearly. Then, I began to add in those other fabrics to see what would happen. I was completely in the zone with no distractions. I added and took away and combined until I knew I had an amazing collection. I distinctly remember feeling so much joy as I let go of expectations and just brainstormed. It was exhilarating.

In the spring of 2022, Elyce Arons, cofounder of the lifestyle brand Frances Valentine, asked if I wanted to use their amazing fabrics on my chairs for a summer collaboration. These fabrics consisted of bold florals and stripes in green, orange, and yellow with a few other minor colors, but no pink. Pink is my signature color, so I began to brainstorm ways to bring pink into this collaboration. I was stumped; no other fabrics I tried to coordinate into the mix seemed to work. When I finally stopped striving and embraced the colors before me, the design came together perfectly with green painted chairs.

Have you ever been out on a walk, on a drive, or in the shower and thought of an amazing idea? This doesn't happen by accident. Your brain is always working in the background to solve problems; you just need to put yourself in the right situation to receive those creative solutions.

Knowing how to come up with a lot of ideas— as well as flesh out the best ones—is helpful for growing your ability to think creatively.

That's brainstorming!

And if you use the steps for doing it well, you will not only come away with great ideas, you will also work toward building your creative thinking capacity.

Anything *goes*

How to Brainstorm

When I taught elementary students in the classroom and worked as an educational consultant with adults, I taught these audiences how to brainstorm ideas. You are never too old or too young to learn the steps for coming up with great ideas. Brainstorming can be done in groups, individually, or a hybrid of the two. Sometimes the ideas just seem to pop off the page, and other times, it takes a while to produce a good one. But one thing is for certain: the steps eventually work to bring about good ideas.

MY RULES FOR BRAINSTORMING

 Block all distractions.

 Write everything down; don't overthink it.

 No judgments at first.

 Outrageous ideas are good!

With these rules in mind, follow the steps below to get your best ideas:

1. GATHER IDEAS WITH NO JUDGMENT

Depending on what I'm trying to brainstorm, this step can vary. If I'm brainstorming certain fabrics for a client, I gather a ton of fabrics in my arms. Usually I'm looking for a certain color scheme or pattern. I get as many fabrics as I can find and lay them out on a table or flat space, and I take pictures of them.

If I'm just trying to come up with ideas, I either use chart paper or sticky notes. If it's chart paper, I draw a web and write down words that answer the question I'm after. As an alternative, I take sticky notes and write down each idea, one per sheet.

My goal is to generate as many ideas as I can, without judging them or telling myself, "That's not a good one." Anything goes! The more outrageous the idea, the better. You can always tone down a wild idea, but quite often it turns out to be the best one of all!

2. GIVE SPACE FOR THE IDEAS TO INCUBATE

I'll hang up my brainstorming paper or place it on a table where I know I'll pass by it several times a day. Then, when I walk away from the design or problem to think for a while, I'll come back with more ideas, often better ones, to add to the paper. If it's pictures of fabrics, I'll revisit them and browse through them several times as I ponder possibilities.

3. JUDGE, RANK, AND ELIMINATE IDEAS

When I'm working with fabrics, I begin to remove ones that I don't absolutely love. I rank the remaining fabrics according to the desired look, and let go of fabrics that don't best fit the project. My goal is to get it down to the three, then two, and finally the best fabric.

If I'm looking at ideas that I've written, I begin to X off the ones that don't fit well and circle the ones that do. Maybe I even combine two or three of the ideas to make a new one. Or, I take an outlandish idea and tone it down.

4. ALLOW TIME UNTIL THE ANSWER APPEARS

If I allow enough time, the right answer always appears. Once I make a design decision, I'm sure of it. There's no wavering. This is the result of giving myself time to really think through the best design.

If I need the right words or ideas for a project I'm working on, and if I take the time to follow these steps, I'll get the right answer. Most of the time we don't want to wait, think, or "procrastinate." But good ideas are worth taking the time to think through; we need uninterrupted time. Distractions squash our ability to come up with great ideas. I prefer quiet when I'm brainstorming. Other people need instrumental music. Do what works best for you.

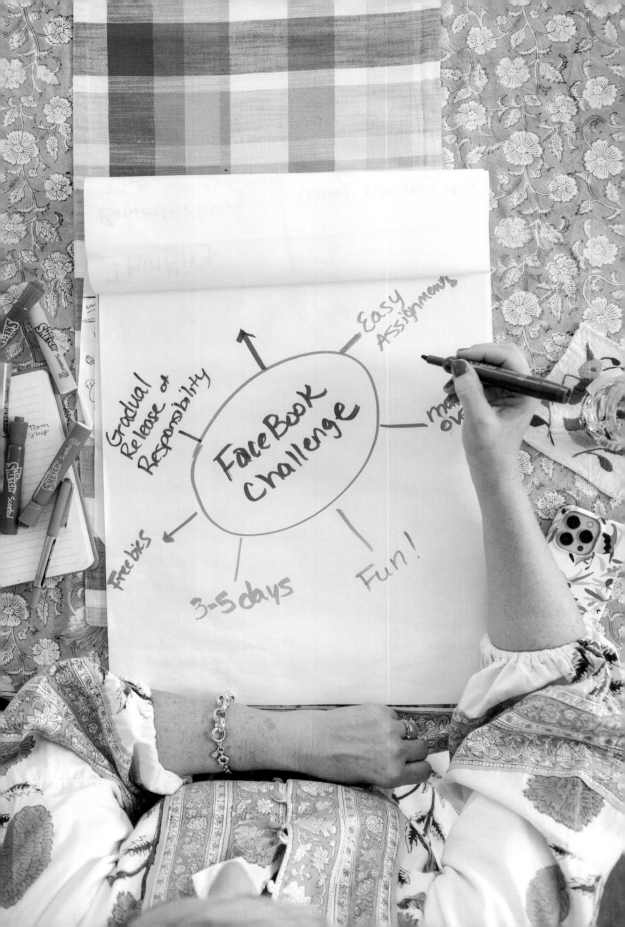

Let Your Mind Wander

A psychologist with a funny-sounding name (Csikszentmihalyi—pronounced "chicks send me high") came up with the idea of flow.

Flow happens when you are so engrossed in something that you lose all sense of time.

When we are in a state of flow, our creativity gets a workout. We can't be in flow all the time, but if we want to build those creative muscles, we should try to experience flow as often as possible. To do that, we have to set the stage for no distractions—which is no easy feat in today's tech-savvy world, but to do this, you have to put your phone away. I like to think about this state as setting aside time for our minds to think and wander.

The easiest way to let your mind wander is to go for a walk in nature or drive with no radio, music, or headphones. I have found that even during my workouts at the gym, I come up with good ideas. The movement helps my brain to produce more ideas. I often have to stop and dictate notes on my phone so I don't forget them. When I need to think of good ideas as I'm getting things done in my workshop, I turn off all distractions—no music, no TV, no phone. The constant noise and reminders stop me from letting my mind wander and come up with new ideas. I also experience flow when I'm mindlessly pulling weeds in my yard or spending time my greenhouse on a Saturday morning.

The key is to intentionally make time to think and plan for mindless activity. If you find that you need music, make sure it's instrumental so that your brain is not distracted by the words of the songs.

WHEN IDEAS BEGIN TO COME, USE ONE OF THE STRATEGIES BELOW (OR ONE THAT WORKS BEST FOR YOU) TO KEEP TRACK OF THESE THOUGHTS.

 Doodle on a pad of paper.

 Write an email to yourself and save it as a draft.

 Draw on chart paper.

 Dictate using the notes app on your phone.

 Record ideas separately on sticky notes.

Think

creatively

Practice Your Thinking

We can train our brains to think differently by practicing our creative thinking. When my girls were young, I would ask questions at the dinner table just to get them thinking in different ways. For example...

If you could have a super power, what would it be?

If you could have dinner with anyone, dead or alive, who would you pick?

What if we had a third arm?

What if (fill in the blank with any event from history) had a different outcome?

How many uses can you think of for a spatula?

These open-ended questions have no right answers. They are designed to get us thinking creatively. These unusual questions make great dinner conversations too.

This practice is no different from what I did as a classroom teacher—my job was to teach my students to be thinkers. We have to be taught to do this and have opportunities to try it; it's not innate for most of us. There are plenty of games that you can buy that have great question prompts like these to help you think more creatively. The more you do this, the better you get at it.

And you will find that it bleeds over into all aspects of your life.

CONCLUSION

Coming up with great ideas doesn't have to be difficult or mysterious. As we practice brainstorming techniques, we are training ourselves to be divergent thinkers. Overtime, this approach to generating ideas will become second nature. Taking time away from technology to let our minds wander will allow us to naturally come up with lots of ideas; we'll be amazed at how many problems get solved as we spend time in nature! And finally, as we practice thinking, we can't help but be the most interesting person in the room.

MY CRAZY, CREATIVE IDEAS:

CHAPTER 3:
Fear of Failing
vs. Fear of

not

trying

Wouldn't it be fun to think of yourself as a creative person? Creative people are not that different from us; they just try a lot of things. They take risks, are more open to new ideas, and are willing to navigate through uncertainty. Most of us are "risk averse"—we don't want to fail, feel uncomfortable, or be disappointed. But the "creativity carrot" is dangling before us, tempting us to walk into these momentary uncomfortable feelings to get to the other side.

The willingness to take risks
is key to producing creative work.
You have to try a lot of things.
So how can we turn our risk aversion into a
willingness to take risks?
I believe it's a mental shift in our thinking.

*We must turn the fear of failing
into the fear of failing to try.*

Try
new
things

What Motivates You?

We all have different motivators that help us take risks and move into the unknown. For some of us, it's misery in our current circumstances. When our misery is greater than the fear of the unknown, then we are forced into taking risks that we probably wouldn't have done otherwise.

Today, Nancy Sargent is an amazing upholsterer, but she had a cushy corporate job for years. When new management took over, she suddenly found herself under a boss who acted like a bully. Her job became so miserable that she finally quit and decided to jump headfirst into learning a new skill—upholstery. She was forced to take that risk, but she gladly did it because her misery was greater than the fear of the unknown.

Regret is another strong motivator that helps us take risks. On our deathbeds, will we feel satisfied with what we tried? It doesn't matter if we failed, but did we at least try? We all know people who die with regrets. Toward the end of my dad's life, he talked about how much he regretted not finishing law school. He was a child of the Depression and grew up poor. He overcame poverty, worked in the insurance business, and raised three kids in a comfortable home. But he died regretting the things he didn't finish.

The thrill of living motivates us too. Something magical happens to our confidence when we try hard things. Getting out of our comfort zone and trying new things builds our confidence and develops grit.

While these new things are difficult to do, the experience is also thrilling because we are trying.

I remember when I first took guitar lessons at age forty. My kids had bought me a guitar for my birthday. I had always complained about how my parents didn't let me pursue it when I was a kid. So I was stuck: I had to learn since they gave me this guitar. I enrolled with a private instructor, and after five months, we had a recital. There was one other adult who was older than me in the recital, and he was really good. The other participants were all kids who were also better than me. I practiced and worked really hard. But when the day of the recital came, and I was waiting for my turn, a mom knocked over my guitar by mistake. I had no idea that would put it out of tune, but when I got up to play a duet with my instructor, my guitar sounded awful. On the one hand I was embarrassed, but on the other hand it was pretty funny. Knowing I survived that built my confidence to try other new things.

The key questions we must ask ourselves:

Will you regret not trying? Or can you live with your life unchanged?

These are good questions to ponder. Will I regret not parachuting out of an airplane? Uh, no. I won't regret missing that experience. But will I regret not taking a chance to be on television if that presents itself to me? Absolutely I will, and so as scary as it seems to be on live TV, I'll take that chance.

Get *messy*

Perfectionism Kills Creativity

One of the biggest hurdles students in my beginner upholstery course need to overcome is perfectionism. Somehow we have believed that perfectionism is the goal of everything we produce... including chairs. Some of us have been conditioned to believe that we won't be accepted or loved if we don't achieve the very best.

But who sets the bar for perfection, anyway?

Most of us are not born with this high standard of perfectionism. We've learned it, accepted it, and taken it on. In the purest form of play, children try things and don't worry about the outcome. They experiment through playing, and we've got to get back to that as adults.

The creative process is messy. If we let go of perfectionism, new experiences can be fun and liberating.

Have I ever made design mistakes on my chairs? You betcha! It's how I learn. But I don't worry about making a mistake when I'm creating. I let my emotions guide me. I think a lot about the design before making my final decisions just to make sure I really love it. If it turns out badly, so what? I'll just repaint, reupholster, redo. I often have to take the risk and try something to see whether it's going to work. If I allowed myself to get hung up on perfectionism with my chairs, I would never attempt any chair design.

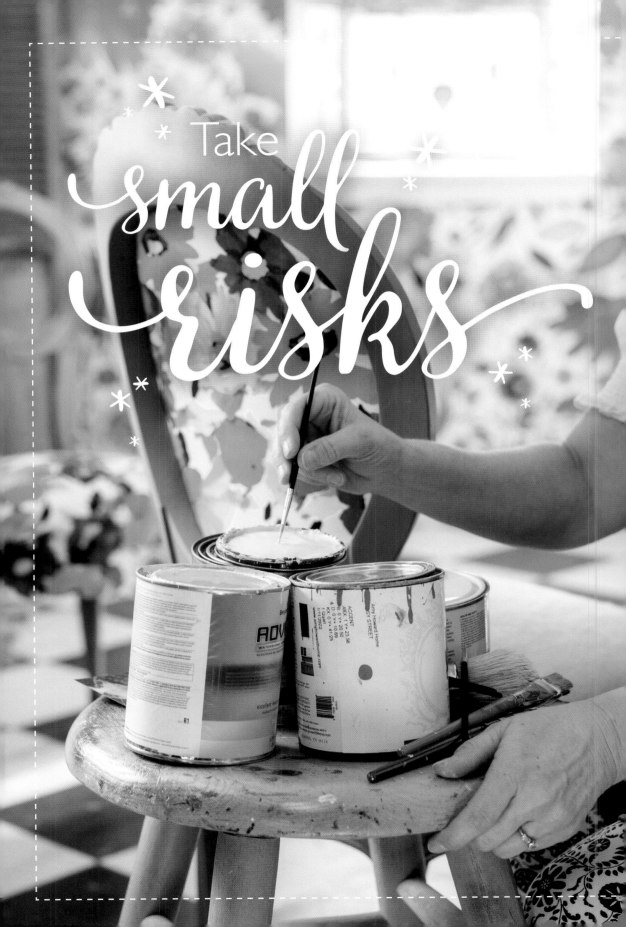

Take *small* *risks*

Build Your Creative Confidence

The way to build your creative confidence is by trying things. Take small risks at first. By doing that, you will realize that you won't die if you fail at something because it's a small risk. Your creative confidence gets built in the process which helps you take on harder and more risky projects. Think of it the same way as building muscle. You don't start out by bench pressing 120 pounds if you've never lifted weights. You start small and build up your muscle over time. In the same way, taking on little challenges builds the muscle of confidence over time. You will see you can do it, and then be more willing to do harder things.

HACKS FOR OVERCOMING FEAR

 Journal your fears. *Just seeing our words on paper can help us explore why we are afraid to step into the unknown. This reflection can empower us to take those risks.*

 Repeat mantras to yourself. *As corny as this sounds, stand in front of your mirror and repeat confidence building mantras like, "I am a creative person," or "I have the courage to try new things."*

 Get around like-minded people. *Creativity spreads, and being around people who think creatively is contagious. It will open new worlds for you.*

 Try small things first. *Success is contagious, and the more you succeed, the more you will be willing to try other new things.*

CONCLUSION

Sometimes there are deeper reasons why we resist taking risks. We might need to involve a professional to help us uncover these deep fears. But the one thing I have learned is that the only way to overcome fear is to face it. I do this by thinking of the worst thing that could happen. Then, I ask myself, *if that happens, how will I respond?* By having a plan, I feel empowered, and I can usually move forward. And 99 percent of the time, those "worst case scenarios" never happen. Becoming a more creative person begins with the way we think.

When we get our mindset in line with who we want to be, creativity follows.

PART 2:

Never stop playing

"The opposite of play is not work—the opposite of play is depression."
—Dr. Brian Sutton-Smith

What does it mean to play? How do you play? *Do* you play? Ask most adults about how they play, and you might get a lot of silence, maybe even pushback. We don't even know what that word, "play," means for adults. As young kids, our days were consumed by play. We learned through play. But halfway through elementary school, we were conditioned to stop playing and be more studious, serious, and well behaved... as if play is not useful after a certain age or is a waste of time. I wholeheartedly disagree with this notion.

Everything we do should start by having more fun. Play is not something we just do on the weekends, or when we can fit it into our schedule. *Play should be a way of life.* Play is an easier concept for adults when you use the word fun. What do you do to have fun? I believe we are all makers, designers, and creators at heart, but many of us suppress it and don't act on it. Being a maker implies we use our hands to make things. Play has a lot to do with using our hands. Dr. Stuart Brown, founder of the National Institute for Play, asserts that playing begins with the hands. Our hands connect us to the brain through play. Through manipulating and touching, we play, and as a result, become happier, smarter, and better problem solvers. ("Serious Play" TED talk, 2008)

You can figure out what play is for you by asking yourself the following questions: What do I do that brings me joy? What am I passionate about? What drives me? The answer to these questions will define how *you* play. Play brings you joy when you do it. It is your passion, your drive.

The following chapters will show how I play through fabrics, patterns, chair styling, decorating, and more. It will explore why our surroundings have a profound effect on our outlook on life. My examples will introduce you to new ways that you can play, too. I play by designing chairs, but others play through gardening, baking, painting, etc. The goal is to explore and figure out your way of playing. Play is the secret weapon to finding your life whimsy.

CHAPTER 4:
Your World
is your
playground

For the past 10 years, I've been driven to decorate my spaces with more color and joy. From my workshop, greenhouse, and home to my car and even my camper, I've been on a mission to create playful surroundings. Why? Because it brings me joy when I spend time in those spaces. And as a result, it makes me more creative.

I find that seeing other's inspiring spaces gives me ideas for my spaces too. Perhaps my spaces will inspire you in the same way.

Let me share those with you.

Fill your
life with
joy
and
whimsy

My Home

I am not a trained interior designer. When designing, my process is messy, and it happens over time. Sometimes it takes a really long time to come together. Everyone's design process is different. For me, I just need to start with one thing, and the design builds piece by piece. I typically get ideas in my head sparked by a piece of furniture, paint, bedding, or wallpaper that I love. And then the design begins to unfold. I add in piece by piece, taking my time.

My home is a constant evolution of ideas that will never be finished. It's my palette where I can express my creativity. I used to dream that my whole house would be perfectly designed. Now, knowing how my process works, I've learned to be content and thrilled with each stage my house experiences. I don't take it too seriously. In a few years, I'll change each room to reflect a new dream or ambition. But for now, I try to live in the moment, allowing each room to bloom.

THE KITCHEN

My kitchen is the true heart of the home and where all our parties take place. It has white cabinets *(someday I might paint them a color!)* and black counter tops. The windows are plentiful, and so that encouraged me to paint my walls a glossy black. That neutral background easily allows for layering color. I always have vases of grocery store flowers throughout the space. I added colorful wallpaper to the back of my lighted cabinets and alongside the paneling next to my refrigerator. The eating area consists of a marble top antique table that I spray-painted gold. My one-hundred-year-old settee is one of the first pieces I upholstered back in 2012, and where I learned to tie springs. The pink paisley fabric of the settee just pops off the black wall and works with the table to create a fun eating space. I am constantly changing out the chairs in this space. I do most of my online work at this table with my laptop as a permanent fixture there. This "office" that I've created is an inspiring place to get my work done. And I've also made my kitchen a fun place to cook too!

THE LIVING ROOM

I purchased some very old French chairs on Craigslist back in 2014, and for whatever reason at that time, couldn't sell them. So I decided to add them to my living room. These chairs are amazingly comfortable for French armchairs, and I'm constantly changing the fabric and paint on them to be the showpieces in the room. After some time, I painted my stained coffee table a light blue after an interior designer friend gave me the idea. My mantle is a place where I layer art depending on my mood and the room's vibe. Salvaged pieces from old homes sprinkled throughout the room add character and uniqueness.

THE DINING ROOM

I've never bought new furniture for my dining room. All the tables I've had are ones I've refinished, and, of course, I've had a revolving door of different chairs that I've used over the years. A large painting by Carrie Schmitt hangs over a buffet that I snatched up from Craigslist years ago. The pale pink painted walls have become the perfect backdrop for a variety of colorful plates, showing off some of my collection.

THE ENTRY WAY

My entryway has a vintage Victorian sofa with a variety of pillows. But the true showpiece are the stair fronts of my staircase that are wallpapered with a whimsical design that I found from an artist on Etsy. I added more Frida paintings my daughter painted for me with colorful antique frames to make each painting unique. Those stairs bring a smile to my face each time I walk up and down them.

THE BEDROOMS

The bedrooms upstairs provide for an exploration of various color schemes. I personally love reimagined antiques and am pretty handy with paint, so I use both of those talents to give my spaces a one-of-a-kind look. One daughter's room is a joyful explosion of green and pink with an amazing floral area rug. An Otomi printed wallpaper provides the whimsical backdrop to a painted antique bed. Antique shutters painted pink hang on her wall on either side of the windows.

My other daughter's room is a celebration of red and pink with other colors mixed in her bedding. Prints include plaid, dots, stripes, and floral as well as the novelty lobster wallpaper in red and pink. An antique headboard painted red finishes off the space nicely.

Blue floral fabric shades were the starting point in my bedroom after years of having white blinds. The room's personality continues with a painted blue bed frame, complementing colorful bed pillows and a pink patterned rug. The room is so large that I added a work table at one end that leads to my upstairs porch. A mantle layered with art provides more color and whimsy to finish off the space. (See pages 47 and 49.)

THE BATHROOM

My bathroom is a spark of color starting with the wallpaper, pink shades, and my blue painted bathtub. The jewelry in the room is the pink chandelier that was handcrafted in San Miguel, Mexico. And the biggest bargain was the mirror I got on Craigslist for $20 and hand painted to match the wallpaper.

THE OUTDOOR SPACE

And let's not forget outdoor living! My front porch has a coffee table, area rug, hanging swing, rocking chairs, and various plants. It's a great place to hang out on nice evenings and chat with my neighbors. My home provides the perfect canvas to express my creativity and playfulness. It's inspiring to sit in every room and dream, reflect, and just live. You can't help but feel like you are having fun just being here. It's the perfect place to play every day.

Learn *as you* play

My Greenhouse

I always dreamed of having a greenhouse. I am a total plant novice, but it's an area where I'm slowly growing my knowledge. The problem was where to put a greenhouse and how to build one. I expressed my dream to Dan, my handy neighbor, who agreed to help me bring my designs to life.

The dream started with purchasing old windows from a warehouse going through a renovation. We got the entire stack on Facebook Marketplace and laid them out on the ground to figure out the length and width of the greenhouse. My garage is full of salvaged materials that I find, not knowing what I'll do with, but all it all has character. I purchased stacks of Victorian shingles a few years before, and once we started this project, I knew I wanted to use those shingles somewhere on my greenhouse. I had purchased an old

Photo by Hector M Sanchez Photography

door for $20 that had been collecting dust for a couple of years. Another neighbor just happened to be renovating a cottage and was throwing out wainscoting dating back more than one hundred years. Of course, I snatched that up! Since I had so many materials stored in my garage, it was a no-brainer to use them in our greenhouse design.

It took about five months to complete the greenhouse, and we designed as we built. I asked if there was any way to make the windows open and close, and Dan figured out a way to add beveled dowels to do just that. I needed another door for the other end, so he took two of the windows and made a Dutch door for me. I wanted scalloped trim along the sides, so he cut down the Victorian shingles to give the greenhouse that added charm. I wanted shelving inside that would collapse if I needed more room, so he built shelves out of cedar with a hinge that could prop them up and easily let them down.

The sun can be brutal here in Texas, so I did not want an opaque roof that would bake my plants. To keep costs low, I opted for a metal corrugated roof which we also used as siding under the windows. Old metal fence posts allow for plants to hang inside. Antique bricks from various locations throughout Texas, St. Louis, and Chicago (all places we've lived), make up the floor. I added vintage-looking lighting inside and out, painting all but one of the fixtures pink. And the cherry on top was an antique rooster weather vane I found at a nearby shop.

The result was better than I had imagined.
And I love playing inside and outside
the greenhouse, decorating and experimenting
with various plants.

I'm learning as I play and being inspired at the same time.

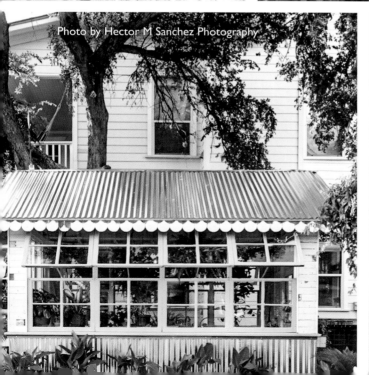

Photo by Hector M Sanchez Photography

Just the
right amount of
Whimsy

My Camper

Back when COVID-19 hit in 2020 and all our travel plans were canceled, I started thinking about how much fun it would be to get a camper so we could travel safely and still see the world around us. I found a used sixteen-foot Shasta camper online, and we drove to the Texas coast to pick it up. It was in great condition, but the brown paneled interior made it dark and uninspiring. I immediately knew I would redecorate the inside.

The design process started with the camel wallpaper and coordinating striped fabric I purchased from the colorful lifestyle brand Katie Kime. My friends at Plush Fabrics used the fabric to design the custom shades with cute scallops along the bottom edge. The vinyl cushions had cracked and worn out, so these were also replaced with red and white vinyl to match the new color scheme. The lush fabric brand Schumacher donated gorgeous fabrics for my new decorative pillows.

I spent a week painting the interior of the camper a bright white, which made all the difference in lightening up the space. Then I spent another week wallpapering the walls. It was tricky, but I did it myself.

From there, the decor was all about finishing touches. The banquet light was rusted, so I replaced it with a blue painted light to match the blue in the shades. I replaced the corroded door handles and hinges with new gold ones. I bought some pink cookware, because, why not? And I found some darling melamine plates created by my artist friend Misha Zadeh. All these little things just add the right amount of whimsy and fun to the inside of the camper.

We named our camper Willie after singer Willie Nelson. It was a symbolic nod to his song, "On the Road Again." And we did get on the road again taking it to local parks, Big Bend National Park, South Padre Island, Colorado, and the Grand Canyon. We learned a lot about the RV life, and it provided a sense of play during a very rough time.

The colorful and playful interior has had much to do with our attitude toward *adding more play and adventure into our lives.*

Embrace *color potential*

My Car

When I purchased my used VW Beetle in the summer of 2021, I knew I wanted to personalize it in some way. I thought about painting it pink. It's my signature color after all and would make for a fun car. But then, I began to think about having a wrap put on the outside of my Beetle. A wrap is cheaper and has more color potential. The only question was, what would the wrap look like?

I put a call out to my artist friends to design a wrap for my car using their art. They provided me with several great mock-ups, and it was really hard to decide. I finally ended up using artist Carrie Schmitt's *Forgiveness* painting. It was one of my favorite prints of hers anyway, and I had used it on my chairs back in 2019.

The result was more amazing than I thought it would be, and surprisingly, my car has made other people just as happy as it makes me. I get called out everywhere I go. People stop me, especially older men, and say how much they love my car. Young kids smile and wave at the car. And women often motion for me to lower my window, so they can tell me how happy my car makes them feel. My Beetle is a testimony on wheels to how color and prints can bring real joy to people.

Set yourself
up for

play

My Workshop

When I found out that Dr. Stuart Brown, the premier researcher on play, works out of his office treehouse, I thought, *Of course he does!* Creating playful environments is key to setting yourself up for more play in your daily life. It made me reflect on my own workspaces.

When I first started doing chairs, I worked on the messy part of stripping them outside in my driveway and garage. (Did I mention how hot the summers are here in Texas?) The upholstery process happened in my bedroom. It wasn't an ideal setup but it worked for the time being. When I finally started taking more chair orders, I had my studio built in my backyard. I took out a small loan—one I knew I could pay off in two years or less. I bought a window unit and a small space heater, but the shop was not insulated so the temperature was never comfortable enough, but it was a start.

I found cheap artworks and old chandeliers, and then I hung fabrics on the walls to inspire me. I used old filing cabinets covered in spray paint, wallpaper, and decoupaged fabric to store my fabrics away. An old armoire stores my paint and other supplies. Over time, I expanded my shop footprint and added in insulation, an air conditioner and heating unit, and more fun decor that inspires me daily.

Your environment is key to producing inspiring work. While it's ideal to have a workshop like mine, not everyone can afford to build one nor has the space. Do the best with what you have. Designate a space in your home, garage, or outside where you will do your work. Then, make it special and visually appealing to you.

The most important thing is to have a designed space to play, even if it means turning your dining room or small corner of a bedroom *into your creative space*.

CONCLUSION

It doesn't take research to know that our spaces affect us deeply. Just experiment with adding color to your space, and see for yourself how your joy increases. Your playful surroundings will encourage your creativity too. Make your home and work spaces a reflection of *you*. Fill them with colors you love. Create spaces that invite you to dream. This extra effort to personalize your spaces provides a big payoff. And maybe you'll find it also brings joy to others.

Farmhouse
Vintage

Classic
Romantic

Black/White
Stripe
gold →

← grainsack

← small floral

Designer's Guild
Amrapali →

WhiteWash

WhiteWash

FIESTA!

SPRING

Winter

BOHO

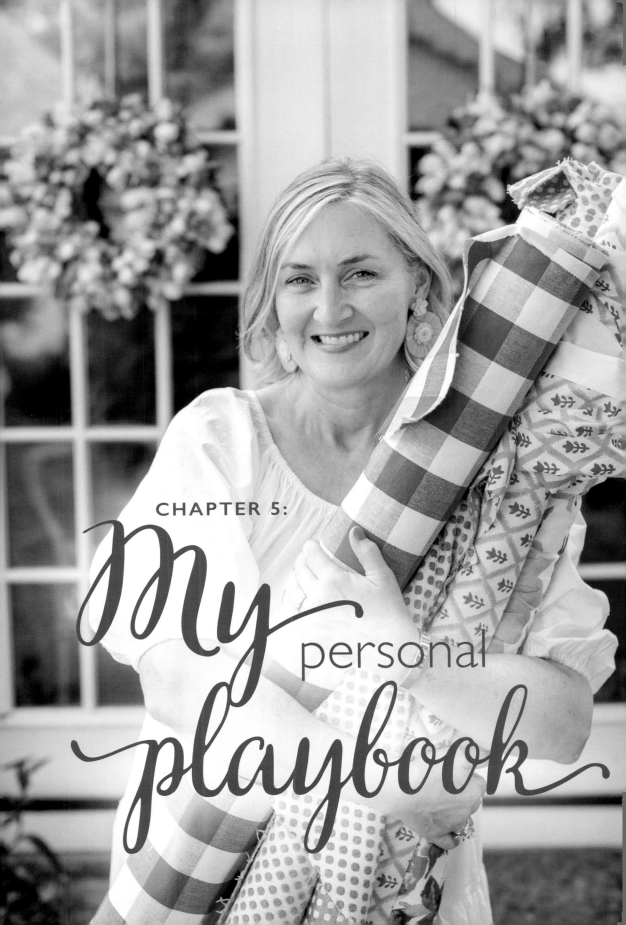

CHAPTER 5:

My personal *playbook*

The most playful thing to me about doing chairs is the designing. I don't necessarily *love* upholstering, but I *do* love designing. For me, doing upholstery is just the means to an end. *Anyone* can quickly learn the steps of upholstery, but developing an eye for design takes time and effort.

When I took my first upholstery courses, I remember looking around the room at other people's projects and realizing that what *I* deemed good style did not come naturally to everyone. Beauty is always in the eye of the beholder, but I noticed that patterned fabric choices could have been better to produce a more stunning outcome. I also observed that fabric placement really made a difference on most chairs. I saw that colorful fabrics were a great way to bring out the charm of antique chairs, but because it was too much of a commitment and risk, my colleagues opted for neutrals instead of color. I became obsessed with using color in my design elements and began my journey experimenting.

I started hunting down antique and vintage chairs on Craigslist to redo. I trained my eye to ignore the stained fabrics, chipped finishes, and the occasional sagging seats with a spring or two sticking out. I only looked at the shape of the chair frame. While everything else can be altered, the shape is the one thing you cannot change on a chair. If I loved the shape, I bought it because I knew I could transform it into something beautiful.

What if I decided that *chairs* could actually *be* art in a room? What if chairs could be the focal point in a space? What if the chairs set the color scheme? I am certain others have done this before, but to me, this was a new idea, a new adventure. As I continued to experiment with designing chairs, I learned how to design a space around the chairs. My room design *started* with the chairs, and the rest of the design complemented my chairs.

Chairs became the art in my rooms.

The

bolder...

...the

better

Colorful Fabrics

The key element that makes my chairs stand out is my choice of fabrics. In my opinion, the bolder, the better. These bold chairs definitely evoke emotion from my followers when I post on social media. And, as I'm working with these colorful fabrics, I experience great joy too.

Available fabric choices just keep getting better and better all the time. Nowadays, there are tons of colorful fabrics to choose from, but most of them are found online. If we look back to more recent history, the '50s, '60s, '70s, and even '80s had plenty of colorful decor inspiration too. Inspiration is everywhere... in our gardens, our clothes (I'm notorious for saying "That blouse would look great on a chair!"), and the more obvious places like Pinterest and magazines.

Right now we are on the other side of the white farmhouse and shabby chic decorating trends, where white dominated home decor. No offense to white! I personally love white because it is the perfect backdrop to layering color throughout a home. You don't even need a lot of color to make a difference when you have white all over. I have a lot of white in my house. White is what makes using various colors work in a home and often on my chairs.

So why do many people shy away from colorful fabrics? It boils down to taking a risk (see chapter 3) and giving yourself permission to embrace the colors you love (see chapter 1). In talking with my upholstery course students, I have found that many of us don't give ourselves permission to love the things we love. We feel insecure about our decorating skills, so we rely on what others tell us is "acceptable" to have in our homes. I've been there too.

And one day it hit me... this is *my house* so why am I so concerned with what *others* think? I should decorate it in a way that makes *me* happy.

If you feel this way, I'm giving you permission to let your home reflect what you really love.

When I'm designing chairs, I start with fabrics. Fabrics, even solid colors, can make a huge impact on chairs in a room. Then, I allow the fabrics on a chair to drive the paint color. I examine the possibilities using paint swatches, take pictures of the combos, and then examine the photos. I look at pictures of the room where the chairs will go to make sure the paint and fabrics complement the space. And if these are dining chairs, I also consider the table. I do a lot of painted chairs, so the paint needs to work with the table. If I visualize the possibilities well, the entire space will make sense in my head. From there, I execute the plan.

Pattern Mixing

One of my signature looks involves using various patterns on sets of chairs. These chairs coordinate, but they don't match. There are a few different ways that I approach pattern mixing across several chairs. Sometimes I start with a color scheme and then find patterns to work within those parameters. Other times I use a "hero fabric"—the most colorful and busy fabric in design—to dictate the patterns in a set of chairs. Then there are times I break all the rules when I mix patterns on chairs.

The starting point is what makes the difference.

Here's
my
process...

DECIDING ON A COLOR SCHEME

When mixing fabrics for chairs, I often start with a color scheme in mind. For example, when I want to use the colors red and pink, I begin by looking for fabrics that have red, pink, or both red and pink. It is okay to have fabrics that introduce another color, but I try to treat those extra colors as neutrals (even though they are not technically neutrals) by accentuating the featured colors with the other chairs.

While looking at my selection, I then look for fabrics that have either different patterns or all the same pattern. I might pick a checkered pattern, a geometric pattern, a stripe, and even a tone on tone floral. I don't want to repeat a pattern too many times unless I'm doing it on purpose.

Next, I have to make sure I have an equal number of fabrics in both red and pink. I don't want too many red fabrics and not enough pink. It is a balancing act until I get the right combination of patterns and colors.

USING A HERO FABRIC

One of the easiest ways to pattern mix is to start with a hero fabric. The hero fabric is typically the most colorful fabric in a room and is often a busy pattern. This colorful fabric sets the color scheme for the space. All the other colors are pulled from colors found in this fabric. The hero fabric sets the rules.

For example, floral fabric makes for a great hero fabric. The goal is to mix other fabrics with patterns and colors to coordinate with this floral. I have to think about doing two things at the same time. For the coordinating fabric, I need a singular color that *also* has a pattern. Quite often this fabric has a neutral color in the background such as white, beige, or natural. That neutral color allows for the main color of that coordinating fabric to pop.

Now I need to balance the colors. I don't want three green fabrics and only one yellow. I either make them all green, or I use a variety of colors taken from that hero fabric. For

example, a hero fabric might have green, yellow, pink, and blue. I can use any of those colors, but I don't have to use them all in my coordinating fabrics. I pick and choose based on what fabrics are available or what colors I want to bring out from the hero fabric.

In creating a coordinated but unique group of chairs, I try not to repeat the patterns across chairs. I want the chairs to have variety, but the patterns need to be balanced. It is okay to do all checks or all stripes, or perhaps two chairs with checks and two chairs with stripes. For example, I wouldn't want to have three chairs with stripe patterns and only one chair with a check. Most of the time, I pick different patterns like a check, stripe, dot, or other geometric pattern. Within these patterns, I either keep them all the same scale, or I make sure to vary the scale of the patterns across the fabrics.

With these considerations, the hero fabric is the beginning and the end of pattern mixing. It determines the rules and sets the color scheme. It is up to me to balance the coordinating fabric colors and patterns.

BREAKING ALL THE RULES

At times, it is fun to break all the rules with pattern mixing, and this usually happens when I have several floral fabrics I want to use together. To do this type of pattern mixing, I need to consider the following two things:

First, there needs to be a common theme color that runs through all the fabrics. It can be any color, but the floral fabrics I tend to choose have the color pink.

Second, the scale of the florals needs to be similar. I find that mixing really large florals with small printed florals does not work as well. I look for florals that are close to the same size because one floral will not outweigh the other. Each flower can hold its own.

When I have the right combination of floral fabrics, I can either cover each chair completely in the floral fabric, or I can bring in other complementary patterns to go with the florals.

Play around

Chair Styling

Back when I first started doing chairs, I struggled with what to call myself. I knew that I *did* upholstery, but the term *upholsterer* didn't truly describe who I was. I designed the look of a chair, but *chair designer* didn't feel right either. After a lot of reflection, I decided that I was a *chair stylist*... I made this title up, but it fits. I styled chairs.

Chair styling is the act of figuring out the right fabrics and looking for a chair or set of chairs. Styling also includes the way the fabric lays on the chair, the position of the print, the type of fabric used, and the welting. The finish of the chair whether it be paint, stain, or raw wood is determined by the fabric and the room where the chair will be placed. The styling of a chair can make or break the end result. The best looks come when I take the time to consider all the possibilities.

Sometimes chair styling can be simply paying attention to getting the check straight on the seat or making the artistic decision to position a check on the diagonal on the backside. If a fabric looks better rotated in either direction or upside down, then I do that. I'm not afraid to use a contrasting welt in another fabric to give it some interest... if the chair needs it. But sometimes simplicity is best. Chair styling is showing judgment, restraint, and a willingness to explore the unusual all at the same time. The chair is the medium to show your artistic style.

Chair styling matters most when I work with floral fabrics. I play around with the fabric to get the best positioning of the flowers. Sometimes this comes quickly and other times it takes a while to decide. I usually have a goal in mind as I style the chair, typically with wanting to showcase a certain flower or group of flowers.

Here are my best tips for styling with florals

(There are always exceptions to every rule!):

- -

1. Avoid positioning flowers smack dab in the middle.

- -

2. Position large flowers to one side, and move either slightly up or down.

- -

3. Consider having extra large flowers peek in from an edge.

- -

4. Don't be afraid to *not* show the entire flower.

- -

5. Try many different positions before deciding.

If you are lucky enough to start with a blank room, then the chairs can lead the design and determine the vibe of the room. But if there is already a table, rug, or other decor, I have to pay attention to it and work to complement it with the chairs. When working on dining room chairs, I have to consider the table, and that leads me to what fabrics and finish I'll need for the chairs. Sometimes, I have to think of these two things at the same time. I select fabrics that can work with a certain finish, so the chairs will look amazing with the table.

But most of the time, I pick the fabrics and then let those fabrics drive the paint color. I do this by putting the fabric on a flat surface and laying different paint color samples on top of it. I take pictures of it and analyze them before deciding.

I am a huge fan of painted chairs, primarily because the antique and vintage chairs I work with have been well used. It is difficult to sand off finishes and hide repairs, so paint is often the natural choice. At the beginning of my chair styling days, I sprayed my chairs. But I had a problem with touch-ups once the upholstery was complete. It was difficult to touch up my chairs and not get paint on the fabric, so as a result, I have embraced hand painting for my chairs.

In short, chair styling is being thoughtful about how the fabric, welt, and finish work together on a chair to give it the very best look for the space.

By taking time to think through the possibilities and play around with the fabric placement, you can achieve a dynamic look for your chairs.

Hunting for Fabrics

The number one question I get all the time is, "Where do you get your fabrics?" My canned answer is, "Everywhere!" That is true. I hunt online as well as at the trade showrooms. I look in antique shops and fabric stores. I'm always thinking about how the different fabrics I see will look on chairs. I'm obsessed with fabrics, and it's a big part of how I play—imagining the possibilities of designing chairs.

Nowadays, fabric shops are few and far between. The online shopping world has drastically affected their viability. Most have closed, but you can still find fabrics at Calico, Hobby Lobby, JOANN Fabrics, and small boutique shops. Boutique fabric shops are my favorite places to shop. There is nothing like being able to see and feel the fabrics in person.

If you have a sales tax ID number, you can get fabrics at the trade showrooms for wholesale prices. It typically involves submitting an application. And most fabric companies also have online components where you can order samples and submit orders.

But, even if you don't have access to the trade showrooms, you can still find many designer fabrics online. The key is knowing the name of the fabric you are looking for so you can search online for it. One of the best ways to stay informed about designer fabrics is to get on their email lists. That way you can gather information about the fabric collections and learn the names of specific fabrics. Quite often, these fabrics are available through various sellers on Etsy and eBay. Other online companies carry designer fabrics at discounted prices along with free shipping when ordering a minimum amount. It may not be wholesale prices, but it comes pretty close.

My favorite things to look for online are authentic textiles, and eBay is a gold mine for finding these. By having a playful attitude and being open to using unusual textiles like bedspreads, tablecloths, table runners, and wall hangings, I've created some amazing chairs, many of which have hand embroidery. I use table runners from Mexico, embroidered by women who are supporting their families. Velvet wall hangings that make fabulous tops for my chairs come from Uzbekistan. Colorful Suzani embroidery from India, meant for bedding, makes interesting upholstery for chairs. I use Otomi pillowcases and tablecloths from Mexico to give my chairs a festive look.

And the best part is that many of these authentic textiles are not super expensive compared to buying fabric by the yard.

My Tips for Finding Great Fabrics Online:

1. Get on fabric companies' email lists—you'll discover the names of the fabrics so you can source elsewhere.

2. Use Google images to find fabrics—sometimes this will aid in your sleuthing.

3. Keep a Pinterest board of favorite fabrics—you'll need a reference for where you found them.

4. Order a sample if possible—it always looks different in person.

5. Spend time searching on eBay—the authentic textiles are plentiful!

More
joy,
less
stress

Upholstery Tips I've Learned the Hard Way

Learning upholstery is not rocket science. Even so, I did make a lot of mistakes at the beginning, even after I took upholstery classes. Based on my mishaps, here are some of my best tips I can pass along to keep you from doing the same.

DON'T FEAR AN ONLINE CLASS

I took my first upholstery course in person, and then had to take it again because I couldn't remember anything despite my copious notes. That can get expensive! Many people have asked me whether I teach in person, but I do not have the space or equipment to accommodate many people. So I did the next best thing... I created an online course to teach beginners. I'm an advocate of learning online because you can rewind and rewatch information as much as you need. And to learn, you *will* need to rewatch because you won't remember all the steps the first few times you do a chair. An online class gives you the opportunity to learn again and again.

START WITH AN EASY CHAIR

I've seen it more times than I can count... people start with very difficult pieces to upholster. (My first piece was a love seat and it's a miracle that I'm still doing chairs!) It is so tempting to take on a hard chair at first, but it tends to bring way more frustration than joy. And oftentimes, people quit before they are done, or they stop after completing that chair because the experience was too difficult. It is hard enough to learn upholstery on a simple chair, but once you get the basics down, those chairs become easy, you get faster, and your skills improve. *And you'll experience a ton more joy working on your projects!*

TRY OUT A LOT OF FABRICS

Take your time when deciding on fabrics. Rushing a fabric choice most always results in a design mistake. I often have to think about the fabrics for several days. Make sure to always get fabric samples when designing your chairs. Fabrics look very different online (and in the store) than when you get them home. When possible, get a sample. Lay the sample across the chair, look at it, and think about it. Try to visualize how the fabric will look on the entire chair before deciding. This will save you from buying fabrics you will never use.

LET THE FABRIC DRIVE THE PAINT COLOR

It is much harder to match fabric to a paint color than the other way around. There are so many different shades of each color, and in extreme cases, you can even mix your own color. But fabrics are not as varied in colors. First, pick your fabrics, and then decide on the paint or other finish.

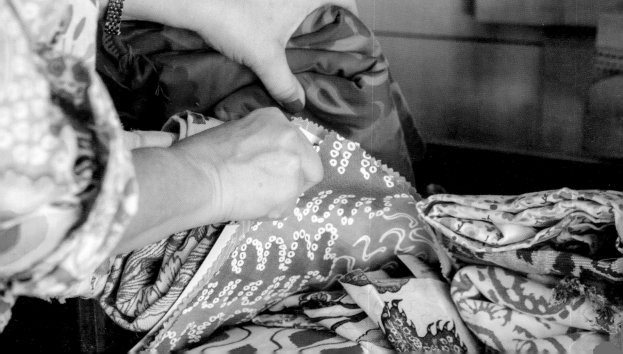

USE A STURDY FABRIC ON THE INSIDE OF THE TOP BACK

When upholstering the back of a chair, you will need material that is sturdy enough to keep the foam from bulging out the backside. To accomplish this, I use a separate fabric inside the top. First, I staple the fabric that is seen on the backside of the chair. Then, I use a sturdy, typically white or neutral fabric next. This fabric often has a gentle stretch to it (and sometimes I use burlap). I use that to my advantage and staple it really tight like a drum. That enables me to build up the front of the chair without the foam or cotton bulging through the backside of the fabric. It provides a strong surface to build up the front of the chair.

ANGLE YOUR STAPLES ON TOP

Most beginners will tell you they make the mistake of poking staples through the back of the wood when upholstering the top of the chair. This mistake happens because they either staple too close to the edge of the top, they angle their staples in the wrong direction, or they use staples that are too long. The easiest way to fix this is to not use half inch staples when doing the top of the chair. Use one-fourth inch or three-eighths inch staples instead. Also, take your time and make sure you staple far away from the outside edge. Finally, and most importantly, angle your staple gun as you staple the inside lip. To easily do this, move your body around the chair, angling the staple gun toward your body. By doing this, you will avoid stapling through the backside of the chair.

USE A LOT OF TEMPORARY STAPLES

To get the best placement of fabric, you need to use lots of temporary staples. A temporary staple is one that is angled so it's easy to pull out. It allows you to set the fabric in place without committing to it. Sometimes you will need to move the fabric, and temporary staples make this process less painful. This is especially true on the sides of a chair seat as you work to get it wrinkle-free. The fabric may need to move forward and backward on the seat. Once you have the right placement, the temporary staple is removed and a permanent staple is used.

BUILD UP THE SEAT

To get a super comfortable seat, don't be stingy with the cotton. Use a lot of it evenly all over the seat, and then, little by little, build a soft mound in the middle of the chair. That will produce a nice-looking mounded seat without feeling like you are sitting on a tennis ball.

LEARN TO SEW DOUBLE WELT CORD

I'll start by saying that I cannot sew anything except double welt cord. In fact, I would go to the studio where I learned upholstery to sew my welt cord because, back then, I didn't have my own sewing machine. The studio owners would jokingly call me "Welt Cord Wendy" because that's all I could sew! Learning to sew double welt cord is not hard.

FOLLOW THESE STEPS BELOW

☑ *Start by cutting a 2 inch width strip of fabric long enough for the welt to cover the staples.*

☑ *Cut two pieces of welt cord the same length of the fabric.*

☑ *Fold the fabric from left to right over one cord.*

☑ *Place the other cord to the right of the fold.*

☑ *Fold over right again.*

☑ *Place under the welt cord foot on your machine.*

☑ *Sew down the middle.*

☑ *Trim the excess off the welt cord.*

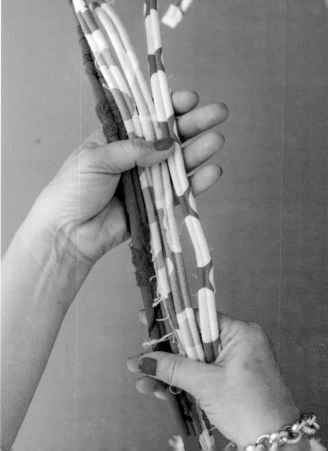

makeover
breakdown

1.

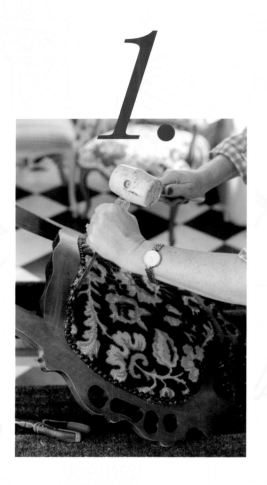

REMOVE ALL THE
DECORATIVE TACKS
OR WELT CORD.

STRIP THE CHAIR
COMPLETELY DOWN
TO THE FRAME.

2.

3.

BUILD THE SEAT BACK
WITH JUTE WEBBING.

WEAVE THE WEBBING
TO MAKE IT STRONG.

4.

5

COVER WITH BURLAP.

STAPLE INTO PLACE.

6.

7.

PILE HIGH WITH
PREMIUM COTTON.

CUT THE 2-INCH
FOAM TO FIT.

8.

9.

COVER WITH DACRON.

10.

STAPLE DACRON ALL AROUND.

11.

FIGURE OUT FABRIC PLACEMENT.

MAKE V-CUTS AND STAPLE ON SEAT FABRIC.

12.

13.

STAPLE BURLAP OR
STURDY FABRIC FOR
THE TOP.

ADD A LITTLE
COTTON.

14.

15.

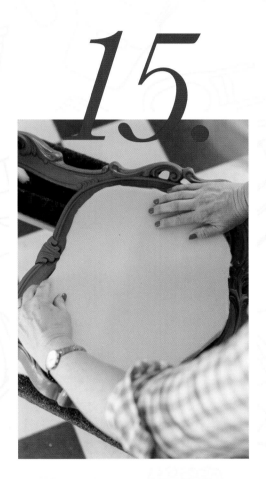

ADD THE 1-INCH
FOAM.

COVER WITH
DACRON.

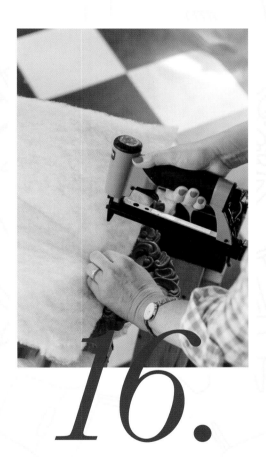

16.

17.

FIGURE OUT FABRIC PLACEMENT.

STAPLE BURLAP OR STURDY FABRIC FOR THE BACKSIDE

(*Some chairs are designed differently).

18.

19.

COVER WITH
DACRON.

FIGURE OUT FABRIC
PLACEMENT FOR THE
BACKSIDE.

20.

21.

SEW THE DOUBLE
WELT CORD.

HOT GLUE THE TRIM
ONTO THE CHAIR.

22.

23.

TUCK IN ALL THE
HANGING THREADS.

THE CHAIR
IS DONE!

24.

CONCLUSION

Chairs are the medium through which I play. My room design process often starts with the chairs—I treat chairs as art in my spaces. I love imagining what a chair can become by giving myself permission to design with colorful fabrics. Sometimes my chair design involves pattern mixing—my signature look. I can pattern mix by starting with a color scheme or a hero fabric. But sometimes I just break all the rules to get a fun, whimsical look. My focus is always on getting the best design for a chair, and the act of chair styling is paramount to that.

Through this journey, I've found places to source great fabrics, and I've also learned some helpful upholstery techniques along the way.

I play the most when a chair makeover is in action; it is the true culmination of how I play.

CHAPTER 6:

The
Power
of
play

Play is a state of mind that one has when absorbed in an activity that provides enjoyment and a suspension of sense of time. And play is self-motivated so you want to do it again and again. (Stuart Brown, *Play*, p. 60)

A few years back, I posted a picture of me golfing during the week. My children reached out and asked what was wrong. It was foreign to them *(and me)* that I would take time off during the work week to goof off. I was so stressed and burned out with work, but I still had to *make myself* go have some fun. At first, I felt guilty and irresponsible—I had way too much to do. But that day, I played, and it didn't take long for me to begin enjoying myself. Time seemed to stand still as I flew around the course in the golf cart hitting ball after ball. I didn't have a worry in the world.

If I'm lucky, I spend the weekend mornings in my greenhouse. I meander around out there, checking on my plants, planting new ones, and rearranging things. I don't really have any particular goal in sight, but I wander around, letting my imagination dream up new ideas for my little outdoor plant house. When I finally look at the clock, I've been so lost just goofing off that I can't believe it's already lunchtime.

Another way I play is taking time to be in nature, whether it's in my pool, sitting on my porch, or taking a long walk along a local trail. It is fun and rejuvenating for me. And it's probably why I love summer the best of all seasons.

Last Christmas, I was inspired by an Instagram post to host a gingerbread house decorating party for a few friends and their adult daughters. Originally intended for children, I decided that the adults in my life could all use some frivolous play. It took hours and hours to prepare the mini houses and royal frosting. I shopped from store to store looking for just the right colorful candy decorations. I went all out on the table set up. I even found some super cute mugs from Anthropologie to give as gifts. One friend, who is not particularly into arts and crafts, said beforehand that she would probably just watch us and not participate. But when the party started, she couldn't resist joining in. (And truthfully, hers turned out to be one of the best ones!) We talked, laughed, decorated, and just lost ourselves in the hours. Play is contagious.

Another way I play is through making cocktails with my husband.

This new adventure in mixology all started back in 2020 when we produced a weekly video to post on social media, "Cocktails with the Conklins." In each episode, my husband, Blane, taught me how to make a cocktail. I don't even have to drink them to have fun mixing them. For me, it's bringing the worlds of art and science together. And as a bonus, we get to do it together!

Here are some of my favorite recipes created by my husband.

The Wendy:

Ingredients:

2 OZ GODIVA CHOCOLATE LIQUOR

1 OZ GRAND MARNIER

Directions:

ADD ICE.

STIR FOR 15 SECONDS.

STRAIN INTO A GLASS.

Magdalena:

Ingredients:
2 OZ TEQUILA
¾ OZ FRESH LEMON JUICE
¾ OZ AGAVE SYRUP
(MIX EQUAL PARTS WARM WATER WITH AGAVE SYRUP)

Directions:
ADD ICE.
SHAKE & STRAIN INTO A GLASS WITH A SUGAR RIM.

The Bluebonnet:

Ingredients:

MUDDLE A HANDFUL OF BLUEBERRIES IN A SHAKER.

ADD 2 OZ VODKA

½ OZ AGAVE SYRUP

(MIX EQUAL PARTS WARM WATER WITH AGAVE SYRUP)

¼ OZ FRESHLY SQUEEZED GRAPEFRUIT JUICE

Directions:

ADD ICE.

SHAKE & STRAIN INTO A GLASS.

GARNISH WITH BLUEBERRIES ON A TOOTHPICK.

When was the last time you played?

What does play look like for you? Play is different for everyone. What may be play for you could be work for someone else. I define play as an activity that allows us to have fun with no goal in mind; it's pure enjoyment. It doesn't necessarily mean that you don't produce something from playing, but it's not the goal.

Most of us don't play as much as we should.

We are too busy working, living, and quite frankly, surviving. Many of us are so detached from who we are and what we enjoy because of life's demands, that we don't even know *how* to start playing more. And when we do know what it means to play, most of us don't do enough of it.

When I hear adults saying they need more hobbies in their life, what I think they are *actually saying* is that they need to take time to play more. Funnily enough, that idea of needing to play more can also become a burdensome task, something else to fit in our busy schedule. And even if it is fun, we feel guilty for taking time out of our busy days to do it. So why do we really need to play? And what does play look like?

Carve out *time* to *play*

Why You Need Play

Do you want to be a more creative person? Carve out time to play. We have all been around people whose playful imagination never seems to run dry from ideas. They appear to be having a great time because they produce such creative work. They do this because they make time for play.

Faced with needing to solve a problem or come up with a good idea? Take a break and play. When we play, we allow our brain to refocus so it can solve problems and think of new ideas. This happens because play gets us to think differently by freeing us from daily habits so we can be more creative. How many times have you thought of a great idea in the shower, on a long quiet walk, or in your dreams? This is the result of taking time away from the stress of daily life to play. New ideas can come during play or later on when you get back to your task. Make no mistake, these ideas are a result of taking time to play.

Photo by Dennah Renee Photography

Well-balanced people make time for play because they realize it makes them healthier, more effective workers, and better friends.

- **PLAY** improves your mental health—Having fun releases endorphins, which reduce stress in our bodies and make us happier. Having fun also keeps us sharp mentally.
- **PLAY** keeps burnout at bay—We release stress when we play and can get back to work refreshed. If we don't include regular play in our lives, we stop achieving at our work, and we eventually face burnout.
- **PLAY** enhances our social life—Playing with others provides opportunities to make new friends, whether it be sports, crafts, cooking, or book clubs. Whatever the "play activity" is, it should be something you enjoy.

When you have downtime to do the things you love doing, you can't help but feel happier. Play has so many more benefits than what's listed above, but these few benefits should be compelling reasons to make time for play.

Be
in the
moment

What is Play?

PLAY IS A MINDSET.

More than anything, play is a mindset. At its essence, it is having a playful approach to life. When we are driven by fear and stress, play is not an option. We find it impossible to play or even understand the meaning of play. And when we *try* to incorporate play, we find that we cannot enjoy it. Everything must have an outcome, and so even activities meant for play become work and cannot be enjoyed. If play is a way you approach life, the result of this mindset makes life more joyful.

PLAY IS AN ACTIVITY.

Play is having fun and doing something that you *want* to do—you are not being made to do it. It can be daydreaming, painting, people watching, swimming in the ocean, or cooking classes. You can learn something or not. There does not *have to be* an outcome or product. The essence of play is pleasure. If you are wondering what play is *for you*, pause and ask yourself, "What do I love doing (or want to do), but rarely make time for?"

PLAY BRINGS ABOUT FLOW.

Positive psychologist Mihaly Csikszentmihalyi coined the term *flow*. Flow happens when you play. Flow is being in the zone, enjoying something so immensely that you lose track of time. You are not constantly checking your watch. You are not checking things off your to-do list. You are in the moment, immersed completely, enjoying yourself.

PLAY ENCOURAGES EXPERIMENTATION.

When kids play, they naturally experiment with things. Their mind is curious and open to new experiences. *What does it feel like to get stuck in mud? How do I like playing this game? What happens when I combine these two colors?* Kids are open-minded to checking out new things. If you want to play more, begin by picking up some toys and experimenting with them. See what happens.

PLAY CAN BE GOOFING OFF.

Playing doesn't *have to be* a specific hobby or task. Play can be what I like to call "goofing off." I play a lot in my greenhouse by just meandering around. I lose track of time and enjoy myself immensely as I experiment with different plants.

TO KNOW IF YOU ARE PLAYING OR NOT, OBSERVE THE SITUATION AND ASK:

✔ *Am I having fun?*

✔ *Does this bring me joy?*

✔ *Does this make me feel like a kid again?*

✔ *Do I lose track of time?*

✔ *Do I want to do it again?*

enjoy yourself

How to Play

If you find that you are not playing as much as you *think* you should, you are not alone. At first, it might take some effort to incorporate more play into your daily routine. Give yourself permission to play. Tell yourself that it's okay to goof off for a while. It's not indulgent to enjoy yourself. Go into it with no expected outcome. First, look at the tips below, and then try my "7-Day Play Everyday Challenge."

TIPS FOR PLAYING MORE

☑ *Set aside a time on your calendar (1- hour minimum per day).*

☑ *Be open to trying new things; you might find something you like.*

☑ *Brainstorm a list of things or places you want to experience.*

☑ *Resist your typical routine.*

☑ *Don't worry about being good at play.*

☑ *Force yourself to stay playing for the entire time allotted.*

7-Day Play Everyday Challenge

DAY 1 — Try something you know you like, but never make time for (explore an antique mall, shop for shoes, redecorate a room).

DAY 2 — Go outside and goof around with no outcome (play in the sand, play in the dirt, walk in nature, lay down and daydream like a kid).

DAY 3 — Eat an unusual new food (not something that grosses you out, but something you are curious about).

DAY 4 — Go somewhere you've been wanting to go but have just put it off (explore a nearby small town, visit a haunted cemetery, or test drive a luxury car).

DAY 5 — Try a new sport (putt a golf ball, play pickleball, join a volleyball game).

DAY 6 — Learn a new craft or skill (it can be in a class or by yourself using YouTube as your teacher).

DAY 7 — Try a new restaurant (even if it's just for dessert and coffee, get out of your routine).

CONCLUSION

Life should be about *living and enjoying* that life. How much do you enjoy your life? Do you allow time for pleasure and fun? Or do you feel guilty when you take time to play? All we need to do is take our cues from children. They constantly seek enjoyment, experiment, and play with no outcome. And during their play, they imagine, create, and problem-solve.

Too often we are reminded that life is fleeting when a good friend or family member passes. Or when someone gets a terminal diagnosis, we wonder why that person spent all their time working and very little time enjoying their life. Here's the good news: You don't need that wake-up call to start enjoying life today.

Now, get to playing!

PART 3:

Choose
your own
work
adventure

Sara McDaniel worked as a teacher, school administrator, and educational sales representative for years. But she longed for more adventure in her work life. When circumstances took her back to Louisiana, she purchased a run-down cottage and restored it to be her forever home. During the restoration, she started her blog and social media accounts, *Simply Southern Cottage*, taking her followers along for the ride. As her online community grew, brands began paying her to promote their products. The Louisiana Office of Tourism hired her as a brand ambassador, and she spent time traveling the state, sharing her adventures with her audience. And when HGTV came to town to film an episode for a series, Sara got to be a narrator for the show. Wouldn't it be fun to have a job like Sara's?

Sara's story happens all over the world. Unfortunately, we often find that work is rigid, dull, or predictable. The truth is life should be an adventure, and a big part of our lives is our work. Why live lives of quiet desperation in our work when we don't have to? Sometimes it's our jobs, but quite often it's our attitude toward our work. Since not everyone has the luxury of working a job that they are passionate about—because some jobs do just pay the bills—the answer might be to bring some creativity into the work you already have. Why not put on a new set of glasses and make our work as fun as possible as we seek to solve problems and invent new ways of doing things?

For others, the challenge of setting up side hustles to see if they can make them fly is enough to bring more whimsy, play, and creativity into their work life. They do their job well, but their real joy comes from taking action on new ideas outside of their regular day job. These side hustles can spark the creativity we crave *and successful ones can also pay for those fun vacations!* Perhaps the best thing about a side hustle is that it can be a great onboarding ramp to giving up the day job.

This is my story. What started as a fun challenge to see if I could sell a few chairs on Etsy sparked the gradual desire to leave my day job to become an entreprenista. And it took me almost six years to make it happen. Along the way, I've learned so many lessons on how to run a creative business that no MBA could have ever taught me.

And just because many of us are fortunate enough to work a "passion job" doesn't mean that every day is filled with roses and champagne. Some days it is still "work" and the quest to keep the fun alive takes effort even in jobs we choose. Whoever said "When you do what you love you'll never work a day in your life" didn't have to sand mahogany chairs in one hundred-degree Texas heat! I digress… but I firmly believe that bringing more whimsy into our work is key to living a fulfilling life.

CHAPTER 7:

Sprinkle
creativity
into your
day job

We don't have to look too far to see people who dread their jobs. I had a front-row seat to this phenomenon as I traveled the country training teachers. It's not hard to spot the participants who disliked their jobs, and their feeling of being trapped can make it worse. Most of us experience this feeling at one time or another in our work lives. Thoughts of hopelessness may make work a daily drudgery.

But work doesn't have to be this way.

So much of everything we feel is because of how we think. By changing our thoughts *(see the first section in this book),* we can change our perception of our work-life. How you address your work life is a conscious decision. It's *your* life—*you* get to decide how you want to live and how you will choose to approach your work. Even in the most restrictive situations, we are still in control of our attitudes. When we truly embrace this choice, we realize we are taking responsibility for how we live *and work* regardless of the type of job we do.

I'M NO COMMUNIST

Bluff

...OUT GUESS
...OUT BLUFF
YOUR
OPPONENTS
TO WIN!

12 DICE
•
4 BEVELED
CUPS WITH
SEE THRU WINDOWS

SCORE CARD
NAME

12¢ THE INCREDIBLE HULK 1 MAY

THE STRANGEST MAN OF ALL TIME!!

IS HE MAN OR MONSTER OR... IS HE BOTH

FANTASY AS YOU LIKE IT!

Approach Each Task as a Challenge

I have always looked at my work to-do lists as a challenge, something to problem-solve and approach in different ways. When I was authoring school curriculum, I consciously decided to make any topic as unexpectedly interesting as possible. I remember being given the task to write a unit on the Cold War. If you grew up when I did, social studies class consisted of reading the boring textbook and answering the questions at the end. It was nowhere near my favorite subject. (I'm sure I'm not alone here!) I took on this Cold War writing task by asking myself: How can I make this fun? And I did.

Through research, I found the first *Incredible Hulk* comic book cover that showed how radiation transformed a scientist into that monstrous creature. eBay had a game called Bluff, showing both Kennedy and Khrushchev playing a betting game on the cover, making light of the Cuban Missile Crisis. I found a Humphrey Bogart poster that proclaimed "I'm no Communist," showing his efforts to skirt the McCarthy hearings and being blacklisted out of Hollywood for good. Combining those primary historical sources made the essential content of the history come alive. Almost everything can be made fun and interesting if we put forth a little effort and take on the challenge of trying. By delving into more interesting and even humorous approaches, we can make our work more enjoyable, if not more fun.

Nick, a lawyer I know, makes his work more exciting by approaching his cases with a creative twist. Instead of only arguing cold, hard, legal precedent in his cases to ensure his client's position, he crafts testimony in a story format to pull at the court's heartstrings, and then follows up by questioning legal precedent. He uses his creativity to present the unfairness of the present law in the case of his clients. In some instances, the laws were changed because of his arguments, and as a result his clients were treated fairly.

Be the Chief

Fun Officer

Spread the Fun

Look for ways to make *your* job exciting. For some people, this might be a tall order, but even the most mainstream jobs have potential because of the chance to connect with other people either as fellow employees or customers. You can make a difference in people's lives, and doing this makes you happier too. Decide you will be the CFO—Chief *Fun* Officer—of your job, putting a smile on other's faces around you.

My dad worked as an insurance agent his entire life. And at times, he had jobs he didn't enjoy. As he got older, he experienced ageism and stopped getting the promotions and job offers. (Growing up as a child of the Depression, he was completely gray/white headed by the time he was twenty-five, which didn't help.) He was good at what he did, and he knew a lot, but was forced to take the lower-level jobs. In some small ways, my dad became the Chief Fun Officer of the office, making it a point to bring in chocolates and other clever things to make the environment enjoyable for all of his colleagues. The older ladies loved him for it, and he enjoyed being there.

Intentionally doing acts of kindness for others, with no expectation in return, is one way to make your work environment enjoyable and meaningful.

LIST THE WAYS YOU CAN DO THIS.

_____

_____

_____

_____

To Do...

- [ ] finish set of 6/photograph 9–
- [ ] Pack up chair–ship! 10–10:30
- [ ] Post on social 10:30–11:15
- [ ] check emails 11:15–12:00

Lunch 12–1

Set a
timer
for each task

Set up Gimmicks for Motivation

Little gimmicks can help us achieve a more enjoyable work life. It all depends on what fires you up mentally.

Here's what I've found works for me:

1. SET SMALL GOALS

For me, nothing is more satisfying than setting a goal and achieving it. If you are the type of person who is motivated by goals, then set them up daily or weekly for your work. It can be as simple as how many papers you will file before lunch, or how many rooms you will organize for the week. The key is to set a goal that is achievable while also providing enough of a challenge. Too often we set unattainable goals, and then we get discouraged when we don't accomplish them. Setting *achievable* goals can keep us from wasting valuable time looking at our phones and scrolling social media.

2. MAKE A CHECKLIST

I personally love a *short* checklist because it feels more attainable. Long lists tend to weigh me down, and then I do nothing. There is a happy medium where you can have daily short lists as well as a running long list that these items are pulled from. Make these short checklists between one and three things that need to be done for the day. What doesn't get done can shift to the next day's list.

3. SET A TIMER

For the mundane tasks, you can give yourself a certain amount of time to finish. A timer on your phone can help keep you on tasks that need to be done, even when you don't really want to do them. A timer helps me think of it as a game, and by making it more fun, I get more done.

If you happen to be the boss at work, lucky you! You have more control over the office atmosphere. Give your team members opportunities to try these things to make office life more enjoyable. Be the leader, and lead by example how people can find fulfillment in the work they do. Research shows that people who love their work environment produce better work, and as a result, are happier at work.* It's a win-win!

HOW TO START BRINGING CREATIVITY TO YOUR DAY JOB (WITHOUT ANYONE NOTICING BUT YOU)

Sometimes people push back when I talk about bringing creativity to their day jobs, worrying that they'll stand out (in a bad way)... Here are four ways you can slip positivity and self-efficacy into your daily routine:

 Look for new ways to solve everyday problems creatively.

 Make it your mission to spread joy to others by what you say and do.

 Plan mini celebrations for others at work.

 Create personal work goals for yourself that give you a sense of accomplishment.

CONCLUSION

I'm not the first one to say this—we have only a finite number of years here on this earth. Make them count, and try to enjoy work as much as you can. Instead of accepting the boring tasks, figure out ways to make everything an interesting challenge to yourself. You'll be more engaged and produce better work results if you do.

Decide to be the Chief Fun Officer of your work environment and spread the joy around. You can make a difference in people's lives. And by doing that, you create your own whimsy and happiness. Finally, figure out how to motivate yourself to accomplish your work. Gimmicks like setting small goals, checklists, and timers will help you to get more done in less time. And the feeling of accomplishment will motivate you to even more success and happiness.

It's a wonderful, glorious cycle.

* (Kohll, A. (2019, January 24) How your office space impacts employee well_being. Forbes. https://www.forbes.com/sites/alankohll/2019/01/24/how-your-office-space-impacts-employee-wellbeing/?sh=32db07ec64f3)

CHAPTER 8:
Side hustle
your way to a
new
career

"Use the weekend to build the life you want instead of trying to escape the life you have." — Jari Roomer

Sara Oliver and her five sisters dreamed of working together in some capacity for years. Her corporate job served her well, and she still had several years to go to get her full retirement benefits. In 2020, Sara learned upholstery and was smitten with the idea of starting a side hustle with her sisters in tow—even if they were only her cheerleaders. Sara's job takes her out of town quite a bit, but she commits her weekends and evenings to taking custom orders from clients, designing her chairs, and shipping them out. Sara has no intention of quitting her day job until retirement, but she's building her side hustle in the meantime and having a ball.

A few years ago my daughter Raegan gave me her version of a Frida painting for Mother's Day. She had played around with painting for a while but never thought much of it. I got another painting for Christmas and my birthday. It started an idea... What if I took those paintings and put them on the back of chairs and called them my Frida Chairs? Before long, I had also added pillows and bags to the mix. Everyone was dying over Raegan's art and soon wanted their own Frida commissioned art.

Side hustles are ways to bring in money—outside of your regular work—where you can try on a new job of your own creation with no deep commitment. It's not your main source of income, so there's no pressure to succeed. And that can make side hustles both fun and challenging in a good way! They are often born from passion projects, just creating art and seeing what happens. And before you know it, people are asking to buy what *only you* can do in *your* particular way.

Sometimes side hustles are accidental and come from needing to solve a problem. And then you realize your brilliant idea turned into a product that could solve problems for others and bring in viable income. Other times, the creation of a side hustle is intentional. You decide you will produce something to sell, be it a service or product.

As I was nearing completion of my second upholstery course, I opened an Etsy shop just to see if I could sell some chairs. It was a fun challenge, not a serious job. I already had a career as an educational consultant and author, and I liked my job. There was no pressure to succeed, and while pressure can be helpful to produce creative things, sometimes no pressure can lead to great outcomes too. Within two weeks, I sold my first chair, and the challenge was on to sell another. I really couldn't believe someone wanted what I made. And that sale was the hook that changed my life. I began to wonder whether customizing chairs could really be a *thing* for me. I knew I liked doing it, but could I earn enough money to support my family? I wasn't sure.

Tips for Setting up a Side Hustles

1. INTENTIONALLY KEEP COSTS LOW; DON'T TAKE ON DEBT.

Side hustles demand keeping costs low. And because of that, they demand little risk. Mistakes come when we spend frivolously on side hustle ideas. Set a low budget, and don't go above it.

- -

2. SET UP A PERSONAL ADVISORY FUN GROUP.

Get outside input from those you trust, especially people outside of your field of work. They often think of things you would never consider. Bounce these ideas off friends and family who support and love you. Creative people will do for you what you can't do for yourself; they provide great ideas and feedback.

- -

3. THINK OF CREATIVE WAYS TO GET YOUR SIDE HUSTLE IN FRONT OF PEOPLE.

Enjoy the freedom to do business your own way. Since it is your work, you get to spread the word any way you want. Be unconventional so you can stand out, and pay attention to how people respond.

Your future successes
are determined
by your
past
successes

Taking Your Side Hustle to the Next Level

Side hustles can be a great onboarding ramp to quitting the day job. It's usually not wise to just quit a job when you need the income. The gradual building of your business over time can set you up for future success to transition.

Pretty soon, after I had sold my first few chairs on Etsy, the spark to leave my day job began to grow. I remember sitting on the side of the bed telling my husband that I *knew* I could do this, but I felt trapped by having to split my time and energy between two jobs. If I could only focus on *the* one job, I had enough hope that I could make it fly. The confidence was there because I saw how my early clients loved my work, but the money was not.

I kept working at my day job for almost six years. My family depended on me to bring in money, and despite my husband's encouragement to quit my day job, my greatest fear was letting my family down. If I failed to produce, we would lose our house and probably many other things. It was this fear of failure that kept me paralyzed and in my job for so long.

Failure is something that we are all bound to experience at one time or another. However, the fear of failure *can* often be worse than the failure itself... but I'm not 100 percent sure about this because I didn't fail in a catastrophic way; only in small ways, which I'll soon tell you about.

During these years, I experienced a lot of unhappiness and dissatisfaction with life. I remember one Sunday evening watching a *60 Minutes* story about an artist. This artist made the comment that he will never be happy and satisfied with where he is; he's always longing for the next thing. I turned to my husband and said, "I understand him. That's how I feel." Looking back now it breaks my heart to see that I spent so many years in this miserable cycle, not being present, and not appreciating what I had. It was a mindset problem, but I didn't understand that at the time.

My misery became so great that I booked some sessions with a therapist I had worked with previously. I poured out my heart to her, telling her how I wanted to quit my job, but that I felt trapped because of the money. She told me that I would be successful at whatever new venture I decided to start. Incredulously, I asked her why she said that. I didn't need another cheerleader in my corner... I needed the truth. I needed hard facts. My family's success or failure depended on it. Then she said something I'll never forget. "I know this because your future successes are determined by your past successes. You've been successful in your past careers. You've got it in you to figure this out. That's how I know." I can't begin to explain the profound effect her words had on me. I clung to those words because I didn't have the faith to believe in myself at that time. I needed an outside, unbiased person to tell me that I could do this based on facts. And she gave that to me.

CHANCES ARE,
YOU DON'T NEED MORE EDUCATION

At the time, I mistakenly thought that I needed to be an interior designer, because who does *just* chairs? I booked a meeting with the dean of architecture and interior design at the University of Texas, thinking I needed to go back to school to get another master's degree so I could do what I loved for my job. I asked her if any students in the program also worked a job while attending school because I knew I couldn't quit my job to go to school. The answer was no. That single word closed the book on this pathway.

I also visited an art college with the hopes of taking some classes, just to take some action toward my goal. I got into the paperwork before realizing the school also demanded me to attend full-time. I couldn't just pick and choose the classes a little at a time to fit my schedule. Then, the young man from the admissions office showed me around campus, and we talked about my "little chair business." I was almost embarrassed to tell him about it, but he was so impressed. Maybe I wasn't too far off. Maybe I sort of knew something. Maybe I was ahead of the game, and *I didn't even know it.*

JUST TAKE SOME ACTION

I enrolled in a couple of drawing classes in the local community college as a student at large. I thought that if I were going to do interior design (I didn't yet believe creating chairs was a viable option), I needed to be able to draw. Drawing is hard! It was also fun, and the boost I felt by taking some action toward my goal was exhilarating. I found a few other courses specializing in interior sketching and loved those. Again, I shared about my little chair business, and my classmates appeared to be impressed. This was another clue and boost to my confidence that I might be on the right path. I continued taking chair orders, and my schedule filled up leaving no free time outside of work.

GET SOME SKIN IN THE GAME

Around this time a mutual friend introduced me to a local businesswoman named Vera who became my mentor. We met every three months or so at a local coffee shop for an hour. I paid her $100 every time we met, which was a lot of money to me at the time. It had to be worth it to her to help me. It also had to cost me something for me to take it seriously. I came prepared to every meeting with a long list of questions, ideas, and problems.

I remember one meeting when I was feeling particularly low. Sales were dismal, and I had just refunded the one little sale that I had made. I broke down sobbing at the table. The reality of leaving my day job seemed impossible if I couldn't make enough money. Vera assured me that there was a net waiting to catch me, even though I couldn't see it. I'm not sure whether she was telling me the truth or not, but I desperately needed to hear those words of encouragement.

Working two full-time jobs is not for the fainthearted.

Every meeting I would slide into my chair and say, "I've got to figure out a way to quit my job." One day, Vera took me up on this question and presented me with a challenge. *Take a six-month leave of absence from my job along with a small loan to help pay the bills.*

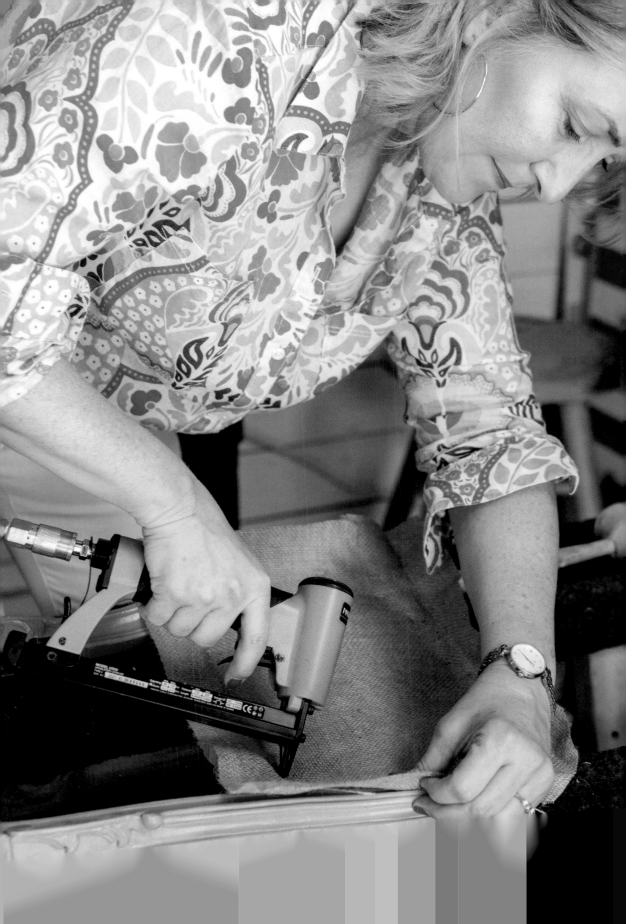

BET ON YOURSELF

There is a fine line between taking the jump and knowing for sure it's going to work. You don't know *for sure*. You'll *never* know for sure. There is risk involved. Sometimes you have to bet on yourself. I thought about my therapist's words from a few years before. Vera's challenge to take this six-month leave of absence frightened me. Would I really commit to this new chair venture and throw myself in 100 percent?

I went home and timidly told my husband what she said. His response: "What do you think about it?" I honestly told him that it scared me. And truth be told, I'm sure it scared him too. Neither of us liked the idea of taking on debt.

But my misery was greater than my fear of the unknown. So I jumped.

FEAR OF FAILURE IS NOT YOUR ENEMY

One thing I underestimated when I took my side hustle full-time was the level of fear that comes along with it. No matter how successful my side hustle became, the idea of not having the security blanket of a "secure" paycheck caused me to think so many irrational things about myself, like *Could I really make money doing this?* (Even though, at some point, I was making more money doing it than when I was training teachers.)

The only way I could break free from the fear paralysis was to face the worst possible scenario and figure out what I would do if that happened. *What is the worst thing that could happen to you?* For me, it was losing my house. I dreaded the thought of having to tell my teenage daughters and husband that I just couldn't make enough to contribute to our monthly bills. And that our largest bill—our mortgage—would be the one that we would have to cut. What would I do if that happened? I consciously decided it wouldn't be the end of the world for me if that happened. I *decided* that I would just get another smaller house and make it cute for us. I still didn't *want* it to happen, but I had an answer for what I would do if it did. Everyone lives with different circumstances, and we all have to decide what we can afford to lose or what level of risk we can tolerate. This happened to be the risk I was willing to tolerate.

The decision to leave a day job should be thought out. It is a serious decision. The fear will always be there, so don't wait for the fear to go away. It takes courage to move ahead in spite of the fear of the unknown. Most likely, you will need to work in your day job for a while, so make it your mission to add joy (see chapter 7) to that day job to make it more bearable.

There is one truth I've observed for those who *do* move forward. Their misery in their current job was greater than their fear of the unknown. The day job becomes intolerable. My job as an educational consultant required a lot from me. Writing books and training teachers demanded my focus and effort. And I was good at it. The guilt I felt over not wanting to do this job was overwhelming. *Why couldn't I be satisfied and happy? Most people would kill for a job like this.* But I was miserable. I learned how to bottle up the misery and dissatisfaction so that I could still give 100 percent to my job. The schools, teachers, and students deserved that. And every other spare moment was used up building my chair business and fulfilling orders. I never had weekends off or evenings to myself.

The fear of failure can be quite motivating. *How badly do you want this? Are you willing to give this everything you've got?* I told my boss I needed to take a six month leave of absence for personal reasons. Two days into that temporary leave of absence, I knew I would never go back. I felt like a weight had lifted off of me, and I could finally focus on my business—giving 100 percent to working on chairs. I threw myself into the work wholeheartedly.

Did I still have fear? You better believe I did! At first, I would wake up in the middle of the night thinking, *What have I done?* But I used that fear to motivate me to work hard and try new things in my businesses.

In the midst of this anxiety,
I also experienced a level of happiness
that I had never known before.

Tips for Working Two Full-Time Jobs

It's hard to split your thoughts and time when you are trying to transition from your day job to your passion job. This is especially hard when your day job is demanding and requires all of you. I've traveled this road, and I found a few things that helped me during this process.

COMPARTMENTALIZE

To manage this tricky situation of working two jobs, you must compartmentalize to make it work. Set your day job work hours and your creative work hours, and stick to them. Don't mingle the two. This will require discipline. You won't *want* to work your day job, but you *have to* for a while. And the reality is you will have to sacrifice time during the evenings and weekends for your passion job, but how deeply do you want it? This is the real test to see if you have what it takes to make the switch.

EMBRACE WORKING HARDER

My friend Sara from *Simply Southern Cottage* likes to say, "I quit my forty-hour-week job to work eighty hours, and I've never been happier." When you work for yourself as an entreprenista, you typically work way more hours and *much harder* because the buck stops with you. It's up to *you* to make the money. I used to wake up every day worrying about making enough to provide for my family. And somewhere along the way, I stopped worrying about that. I had set up enough streams of income through both my courses and chair sales to provide for my basic needs.

START NOW, START SMALL

When spring of 2020 came around, I had spent eight years building my business, and only two of those years were full-time doing chairs. I had a good framework in place for my business. COVID-19 had caused many businesses to lay off their employees, and my previous job was no exception. I woke to the news that the majority of their staff had been let go. That news shook me to my core. I would have been among those let go. And we would have lost our house and many other things. It would have *devastated* my family. However, I had done the hard work, laid the foundation, and built my own future. It had taken years and a lot of hours, but it was worth it. I am my own job security. My ability to make money is in my control, not someone else's. I started as a small side hustle business, and I built it little by little into what it is today.

CONCLUSION

If you want to try on a new career, start it as a side hustle first. See if you like it, and if you do, keep your costs low, set up your personal advisory group as your lifeline, and then think of creative ways to get your business in front of people.

And if you do decide to go the side hustle route, know that most of the time you don't need more education if it's only to boost your confidence. Just take some action on your ideas, commit to it by investing in yourself with mentors and coaching groups, and see what happens. When faced with uncertainty, bet on yourself. Use your fear to motivate you to work hard.

If you wait for what you think is the perfect time to start your new business or adventure, it may never come. The perfect time is now. Start small and build it little by little. It is about taking action today. And by taking action, you will be moving toward the life you want for yourself. Over time, you just might be amazed at what you can accomplish.

Photo by Nicole Davidge

CHAPTER 9:
Making It—
Tips from an
entreprenista

"You can fail at what you don't want, so you might as well take a chance on doing what you love." — Jim Carrey

I never dreamed I would be an entrepreneur *(or entreprenista in my case)*. Sure, I was a self-starter, driven, loved a challenge in my work, but I never connected the dots to even *think* those traits would be ideal for starting a business. Furthermore, I didn't have any business experience or training. Why in the world would I start a business? Turns out, those are pretty good traits for being an entreprenista.

In the few years I've been running my business, I've learned so many lessons (and I know there are many more to come). That's part of the reason I love owning a business.

There's always a problem to solve,
something new to learn,
and a challenge to take on.

Here are a few things
that I've learned so far.

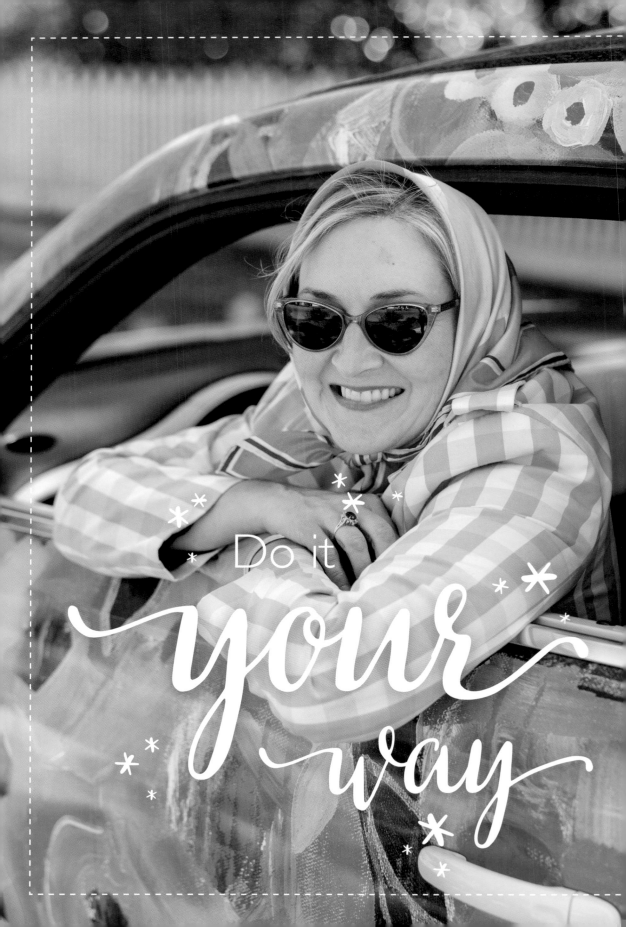

Understand That "Build It, and They Will Come" Is a Lie

A few years into doing chairs, I applied to be a vendor at a high-end flea market. I thought I had made it. I could see full-time chair work in my near future. I set up my large booth with all kinds of chairs, tables, settees, and chandeliers. I put on my cute dress, fixed my hair, and even had food to offer shoppers. I waited anxiously for buyers, but very few came.

There were thousands of people at this venue, but because I was new, I was put on the last row—something I didn't realize when I signed up for this gig. And, unfortunately, not many people ventured back onto that row. I sold enough to break even, and that was heartbreaking. I thought I had failed. But the truth was that I learned flea markets, even high-end ones, are not the right venue if you want to price high enough to make a profit. People who go to flea markets are not planning on buying expensive furniture. They are looking for a deal. This discovery was a hard lesson to learn.

That experience also taught me that selling in person was not the way to go for my business. I had dreamed of owning my own shop one day. But the reality hit me during that week as a vendor that either I would have to dedicate my time to running the shop or hire people to help me. This venture would cost me either my time or my money. And then I would need to pay the overhead of expenses like a lease, utilities, and employee salaries that would eat away at my profit. Selling online was the way to go to keep my expenses at a minimum. This gut feeling was further confirmed when COVID-19 happened, and everything shut down. People with storefronts found themselves with no shoppers, no income, and a big fat lease to pay. You can't just build it and expect people to come; they won't.

ACCEPT THAT YOU DON'T NEED AN MBA

Because I had no business training, I thought I was missing out on how to sell and make money. (No offense to anyone who has an MBA; I admire that.) In fact, I *wanted* that degree. I wasted a lot of time wishing I had an MBA so that I could be successful as an entrepreneur. I felt that there had to be some big secrets that I was missing. And I'm sure there were some. But instead, my situation forced me to rely on my common sense, intuition, and creativity, which turned out to be the best thing ever for my business!

Yes, I made a lot of mistakes, but I also gained a lot of confidence as I figured out how to make enough money. My guiding principle was to keep my eye on the bottom line. Was I making money or losing money? Was I spending too much on frivolous business expenses like business cards? (No one needs those in today's society—just look me up on social media!) In time, I learned to maximize my profits by making smarter, common sense-based decisions.

The lack of any formal business training forced me to think more creatively about my business. To get attention, I hosted "chair parties" to announce and present my new line of chairs. I decked out my house with vignettes of my chairs, planned interactive games to get people excited about my chair business, and even persuaded a local bakery into donating treats.

Instead of blatantly selling my chairs on social media (such as posting a picture and saying it's for sale), I posted details about the chair design, my process, and personal messages to spark happiness in my followers. It's the inside-my-head process of what I do as a maker that interests people. It's getting inside my creative design process as I share my thinking. It's a new world to my audience, and it's fascinating to them. I was selling without "selling the normal way."

I realized my greater purpose in doing chairs was to bring joy to others, whether I sold to them or not.

IGNORE YOUR EGO

Everyone I met would tell me that I should have my own shop. I could tell that was *their* measure of success. It's hard to disappoint people and ignore those expectations. It is even harder when you have people look down on you because you don't do things the "expected way" for a business.

This may just be your ego talking, and you may need to rechannel it. In my experience, it doesn't matter what others think about your business; what matters is your bottom line. Are you making enough money that you can take home to help your family? Are you happy running this business? Is it satisfying *to you*? Are you making a difference in people's lives? These are the things that I find truly matter.

Just because someone runs a business doesn't mean they are smart. It does mean they have a dream and are willing to take a risk on an idea. But it doesn't mean that they know how to run a business successfully. Without looking at a business's books, you really can't know for sure whether it's profitable.

CHOOSE A NICHE TO STAND OUT

Artist and graphic designer Ashley Ward creates handcrafted art made with sustainable materials. She tried many different ways to sell her art including T-shirts, cards, and bags, and while these sold decently, none of them were taking off. And if her products sold, she would have become a shipping fulfillment center... something she didn't want to spend her time doing. To really make her mark *and* make money, she realized she needed to niche further into doing oversized pieces of wall art instead. Her black-and-white style of graphic art perfectly suits large statement pieces. Ashley's decision was a good one for her because it allowed her to focus and be known for one thing.

Deciding to niche is a scary thing. Niche means to specialize one's offerings, to hone down to a small sliver of a pie and leave the rest behind. Most people refuse to niche down because of fear. They want to serve everyone, not just a small slice of the population. *Why close a door to selling to everyone?*

Because when you try to be everything to everyone, you end up being nothing to no one.

During my unhappy years when I was seeing a therapist, I mistakenly believed I needed to be an interior designer... because who does *just chairs*? *That* would be unconventional and weird. I had no idea I had a goldmine niche sitting in my lap. Niching into chairs was exactly the way to stand out. But it took me a while to completely understand and embrace this stance.

In time, I learned that it's not *good enough* to just niche into merely chairs. My personal taste of the style of chairs I do, the way I style each chair, the fabrics I love—all these elements made my niche more specific. I leaned into my way of doing chairs, and that is what helped me define my niche. It's what helped me to stand out.

The only way to really shine, even if everyone is doing the same thing, is to do it your way. You have heard the saying, "You do you." It takes bravery to fully show yourself in your work. The fear of rejection is always there. *What if people don't like this? What if they think I'm weird? Am I good enough?* Everyone wonders these things at one time or another.

The way to push past those insecurities is to listen to your inner voice and ask, "What makes me happy in my work when I'm expressing my truest self?" Follow that lead. Decide not to worry about what others think when you create. You will never please everyone. And those who don't like your art are not your people anyway.

VALUE YOUR WORK

For almost six years, I worked toward my goal of quitting my day job by working nights and evenings on my chairs. But I could have gotten there sooner if I had been smarter on pricing my chairs.

At first, if I only made $100 profit on a chair, I was happy. But in reality, that small profit was not worth my time. Like most makers, I thought more about what people would be willing to pay for my chairs rather than what they were really worth. Even though my husband encouraged me to quit my day job early on, I knew I couldn't bring in the amount of money we needed on a monthly basis. It was because of my pricing. You cannot make money if you don't charge enough. You will never become profitable if you don't charge enough. You will never be able to quit your day job if you don't charge enough.

You have to make a conscious mindset shift to price your art high. What we choose to buy has everything to do with perceived value. Items that are priced low don't appear as valuable to prospective buyers. We place higher values on expensive items. Think about how you shop and value things. When you see something with a higher price tag—and it's something you love—you want it even more. Whether or not you can afford it is another thing, but the value of the item is in the eye of the buyer.

It takes guts to make money.

If I had priced my chairs higher, I could have quit my day job much earlier. Today, my golden rule for makers is to always price your art higher than what makes you comfortable. If you wonder how to price your art, go higher than your comfort level. If your art is not selling, instead of discounting it, raise the price and see what happens.

It takes both courage and a team of cheerleaders telling you that your work has worth in order for you to act upon it. Let me be that cheerleader for you: your work has worth! And you need to price it to show that worth. I learned this lesson the hard way, and it took me way too long.

BUILD YOUR BRAND OVER TIME

I didn't wake up one day and think, *I'm going to build a brand!* I just wanted to sell some chairs. And when I first opened my Etsy shop, I did what a lot of people do. I had a friend create my very first logo. I was so proud of it.

My first chairs were colorful. In fact, my pink settee was my first and one that I still have at my kitchen table. But I also experimented with neutral grain sacks and cowhides. Clients wanted them, and I needed to make some money. Custom orders were the way to go if I wanted to make money.

cottages & bungalows | cottagesandbungalowsmag.com

130

LEARN MORE ABOUT WENDY, VISIT HER WE...

Wendy Conklin came to a "side ... realization. "While I love the charm and look of antique chairs, they do have a shelf life," she says. Structural problems, for example, can cut short an antique's life. "I started thinking. What if I could create that old charm-ing look but have a brand new chair?"

That epiphany led Conklin to create a line of antique-inspired chairs with all of the charm of antiques but none of their problems.

Available through Conklin's business, Chair Whimsy, the pieces come in one of three frames and in one of five looks. All of the frames are made in Italy from European beech wood and shipped to Conklin, who adds the upholstery in her Round Rock studio. One creation, the Frida (*left*), even features artwork by Conklin's daughter Raegan.

The pieces, which retail for $1,199, typically have bold and colorful upholstery, but all of the chairs can be customized.

Says Conklin, "I believe the chairs can be the really big pop in a room." *Chair Whimsy, chairwhimsy.com*

Tour Time

The Austin Modern Home Tour returns for its 11th edition on Feb. 23, but this year's event offers something the past ones haven't.

While the tour will feature its usual array of new and renovated modern homes—including projects from Matt Fajkus Architecture (*left*), Barley|Pfeiffer Architecture, Cornerstone Architects and MJ Neal

Architects, among others—burglars will also get to walk through some mid-century modern homes in Leander.

Tickets for the tour are $15 for children between ages 13 and 17, $40 for adults. Day-of tickets cost $50. *Austin Modern Home Tour, modernhometouraustin.com*

10 SPRING 2019 · AUSTIN HOME

From flipping furni... blankets to hosting... women have found... hobbies into seria... secrets so you ca...

reup...

"About 10 years ago, ...ing as a teacher, I took a coup... upholstery courses for fun. I reup-holstered a few chairs that I found on Craigslist and, on a whim, opened an Etsy shop to see if I could sell them—and sold two immediately! With more requests, I decide to launch a side business, Chair Whimsy.

"To spread the word, I posted on social media, started a website (ChairWhimsy.com) and grew an email list. I sourced designer fabrics directly from textile companies and online from places like Mexico, the Middle East or eBay. Some chairs I buy are new, while others are antique or vintage. When I work with new clients, I look at phot...

Alexis Priddy, 42, Waco, TX

photo... custom labels... woodworking and is u...

"I earn up to $1,200 a month hosting book eve...

"Reading has been a lifelong hobby and brings me so much joy. I've

tidbits about their lives. Then, the audience get...

[house tours]

Genius FLAIR

FABULOUSLY CUSTOMIZED

Clever projects fill a home in Austin, TX, with quirk.

Of course ... couple's ... old Bost... has a ch... name: N... in the G... goddes... first do... Zeus).

$$$ Cash in this week!

"I make up to $14,000 a month refurbishing chairs!"

Here's how Wendy Conklin turned her love for design into a lucrative...

"After taking an upholstery course in 2012, I was hooked. Chairs quickly became my favorite medium...

I learned everything I could about marketing...

henever Wendy Conklin is clothes ...opping, she ...same

I soon figured out that most buyers limit their imaginations, and it was my job to help them visualize what the chairs could become. I began to fill my Etsy shop with pictures of my completed projects instead of just the ugly chairs that needed a makeover. I wrote descriptions that explained the chairs in the picture were already sold, but I could customize something unique just for them. Most people don't take the time to read, so it required many conversations back and forth to help potential clients understand what I could do for them. It paid off. Little by little, I began to take custom orders, and my time filled up. And as I got booked, my prices went up too. At the same time I was taking orders, I was also developing and practicing my style.

Brands are built over time.

Each one needs to begin somewhere.

It takes time to figure out who you are as a business, and what you really do best. All of this should stem from expressing your truest self. I believe brands are best built when a creator leans into what she loves. The only real way to stand out is to be you. No one can be *you* as good as *you* can. It took me a while to understand this fundamental lesson and to confidently move forward.

There's a fine line between balancing a product that sells against doing what you love. On one hand, your product or service should be something people actually want or need. Are you offering something that helps people? Are you good at what you do? On the other hand, I like to think that there is a client for everything and everyone. The key is finding them. And the only way to do that is to produce the work that lights you up inside.

Pay attention to what people say about your brand. You will get emails and messages from people who reach out to tell you what your work means to them. Tuck those comments in a safe place and spend time thinking about them. One card I received from a client, after I completed a set of kitchen chairs for her, thanked me and said every time she walks into her kitchen, she smiles at my chairs. My social media posts are full of what people think of my brand. Many of them say, "Your chairs just make me happy!" One DM told me about a woman's lifelong struggle with depression, saying she looked for my posts every

morning to lift her mood. After receiving these types of comments time after time, I now understand what my brand does for others. I create chairs that bring joy to people. I realize now I don't sell chairs, I sell joy. And people *want* to buy joy.

Your friends and family will tell you about your brand too. Ask them what they think of when they see your creations. Getting outside input is important. When you are involved in your own business, you may not see the forest for the trees. These comments from friendly sources will guide you and give you a better understanding of your brand.

FIND MEANING IN HELPING OTHERS

It is great to make money at what you like doing, but it is more meaningful to make a difference in people's lives. When you create a business that does both, you are very lucky.

I joined my first coaching group back in 2018. My business coach, Tobi Fairley, ran a group for interior designers and creatives. Even though I knew my chairs brought joy to people, I joined Tobi's group because I was at my wit's end. I had tried everything I could imagine to make enough money, and what I was doing just wasn't enough. Tobi's advice to me was to create and design my own personal online course to teach others how to do what I do. I resisted for several reasons:

1) **WHY WOULD I TEACH ALL MY SECRETS TO OTHERS? WOULDN'T I BE RUINING MY CHAIR BUSINESS?** I want *them* to buy *my* chairs! If they knew how to make chairs like mine, it seemed to me that I would be cannibalizing my business. Tobi rationalized that there are people who could never afford to buy my chairs, so why not help them make their own and pay me to learn the process? And, if there were people who would never want to do chairs themselves, they would continue to buy my chairs. Therefore, I had two different audiences to serve.

2) **WHY WOULD PEOPLE WANT TO PAY ME TO LEARN UPHOLSTERY?** They could just look up videos on YouTube and learn for free. It seemed ludicrous to ask people to pay for what they could get for free. Tobi argued that people wanted to learn from me. They liked my style and personal

message. *They actually liked me.* In their eyes, I was a superstar, and they wanted to be in my circle.

3) WHAT RIGHT DID I HAVE TO TEACH OTHERS WHEN I WASN'T THE *ABSOLUTE* BEST?

There were many others who were much better and more experienced upholsterers. Tobi helped me to see that you don't need to be *the best* at something in order to put your flag in the ground and do it. I needed to be good, but being the best upholsterer around was an impossible goal. She knew that my work was good enough for me to teach others. I didn't need to be the best.

4) DID I REALLY WANT TO BE *SEEN* AS JUST AN UPHOLSTERER?

No offense to upholsterers, I highly respect their work. But I wanted to be identified as a designer—a chair stylist. I don't love *doing* upholstery, but the act of upholstery is the means to an end. All I care about is the creative process that leads to the end result. Tobi's attitude was who cares what others think of you, or what they name what you are. If you can serve your customers, and help them live better lives as a result, then you are making a difference.

She convinced me to create my online course, but in my mind, I thought I would prove her wrong. If my course failed, then it would be her fault. Not that I wanted it to fail, or blame the failure on Tobi, but I wanted to protect my ego. The course didn't fail at all! In fact, it made $32K the very first launch. My web designer, copywriter, and I couldn't believe it. Tobi was right, and I was so glad she pushed me to go for it!

The greatest part of creating this online course is knowing all the people I've helped through it. Some participants have been widows looking to redirect their grief into something productive. Others just needed a creative outlet to their boring nine-to-five jobs with some actually quitting those jobs to sell chairs. And during the pandemic, our private Facebook group provided a sense of community and positivity during a very uncertain time.

If it had been up to me, I would not have gone out on a limb and created a course. Fear of failure is a powerful thing that can keep us from doing what we are meant to do.

Shifting our focus to thinking about all the people we will help can help us to refocus our fear and do it anyway.

MAKE YOUR OWN LUCK

Most of the time dreams do not just happen. You have to take positive action to allow them to come to fruition. You make your own luck. I'm not a believer of putting things out into the universe so they can *magically* happen. But I do believe that you should "put things out into the universe," so that others know what you want. Quite often, you'll find a person who knows someone who can make your dreams come true.

My dream was to not just do antique chairs but to also have my own chair line. When people would ask about my work and what I do, I would tell them about my dream. In fact, I spent a lot of time investigating where I could have my own chair frames constructed.

I started with Mexico and tried to source a woodworker there. The language barrier proved to be too difficult. Then, I found a local woodworker who said he could do them. But as time went on, that prospect fell through when the woodworker sold his business and moved away. The man who bought the business also thought he could help me, but that never happened either. As luck would have it, he introduced me to a guy named Chase who had connections overseas.

Chase and I became fast friends. He had worked in the furniture business for years and had even produced his own furniture line. He had several personal connections with woodworking shops in a few different places overseas including Italy. And that is how my dream of producing my own chair line came true.

Tell people your dreams, because quite often, someone knows someone who can make it happen. I could have given up on producing my own chair line idea early on. I remember sitting at my kitchen table when I got the discouraging news that the local woodworker was selling his business. I looked up at my husband and said, "Well, I either give up or keep trying to find someone else."

It would have been easy to give up,
but I chose the harder route and kept trying.

And I'm glad I did.

I made my own luck.

UNDERSTAND THAT BEING IN MAGAZINES WON'T MAKE YOU MONEY

I remember getting the email from an editor at *Cottages & Bungalows* magazine asking if they could do a two-page story on me. I was over the moon! It was my first exposure in a national magazine. I thought I had made it... queue up the chair sales!

They wanted four different pictures of my chairs, and since the article was coming out in the fall, it would be great if a few pictures had a seasonal look. I went to work creating two new chairs and talked my friend into letting me come take pictures at her home, which had a lot of orange in the decor. Armed with only my iPhone and an amazing set of presets that I used to edit my pictures, I worried that my pictures wouldn't be high enough quality. But the publisher loved my pictures, and the spread turned out amazing!

When the issue came out, I expected my chair sales to rise. That phenomenon did not happen. In fact, it's never happened with any of my magazine features including the spread in *HGTV Magazine* in the spring of 2022. Instead of a boost in sales, I found that these features boosted my credibility. And every business needs credibility and validation. My expectations had to adjust—being in a magazine was not going to make me money.

FOCUS ON ONE THING

As an entreprenista, there's always something to do to move your business forward. I constantly have a to-do list written on my phone to keep me organized. The number of tasks that need to get done can be overwhelming for any business owner.

A few years back, one of my friends administered the Clifton Gallup StrengthsFinder assessment. One of my top five strengths is focus. Lucky me! I do have the ability to focus on my work, but when there is a lot to do, I still feel overwhelmed and paralyzed.

To be productive, I first distinguish the big tasks from the small ones. Small tasks can be grouped together. But the ones that take a lot of time need more focus. What works best for me is to do one big thing at a time, get it done well, and then move on to the next task. Time blocking on a calendar helps to keep the ball rolling and helps keep me organized. The small tasks get grouped together, and time is carved out to get them done and off my plate.

By compartmentalizing and setting aside time for all the things, I can keep moving forward and making progress on the big tasks that can take weeks or months to finish. And when I feel overwhelmed, I lean into the knowledge that I am really good and productive when I can focus on one thing at a time.

I apply focus to my business goals.

I set one overarching business goal, and it is very simple: help people while also making money.

For the past couple of years, my main goal has been to get more people into my upholstery course. I have seen firsthand how my course has helped people cope with loss, embrace new beginnings, and find a sense of meaning. It is a way to help people, and at the same time, make me money. The goal of getting more students into my course sets the parameters for everything I do in my business. To accomplish this goal, I have to broaden my audience reach.

Everything I do in my business falls under the umbrella of broadening my reach. Before taking on a new task, I ask, *Does this broaden my reach?* Setting an overarching goal for my business helps keep me and my ideas in check. It keeps me from veering off the path of where I want to go. To reach my goal, I do have to do smaller things and come up with new ideas for my business. This is where the smaller tasks come into play. I need one overarching goal for my business and a few tasks at a time to continue to march toward that goal.

One thing that brings me anxiety is setting business goals that reach way into the future. Having to predict and think into the future puts a lot of pressure on me. When someone asks what my five-year plan is, I have no earthly idea. I don't even know what I really want for my business in two years. My desires can change, and unforeseen opportunities can pop up. I thrive best when I think of my business future in three- to six-month increments. And I limit the number of large tasks knowing that I can only handle one big thing at a time.

LOOK FOR COLLABORATORS

One day, a talented artist named Carrie Schmitt messaged me on Instagram. She asked whether I would be interested in using her paintings on my chairs. One look at Carrie's art, and it was a no-brainer—her painted florals were to die for. I had them printed on cotton, linen, and velvet, and had a ball figuring out the plan for each chair. I paired her florals with checks, vivid colored seats, and various stain and paint finishes. It was the first time I really let myself design with no worry about selling the chairs. Because of that, I produced my best work to that point. I had something unique to sell that others couldn't get—*exclusivity*.

In the fall of 2021, Frances Valentine's co-founder Elyce Arons reached out to me, asking whether I would be interested in collaborating with their brand. The bold floral and striped fabrics arrived, and I eagerly took on the task of designing these chairs. At first, I struggled, trying to pair outside fabrics with these in hopes of getting my signature pink in the mix. But it was useless because it never produced the result I thought it would. When I finally surrendered my chair design to the bold floral consisting of yellow, orange, and green, the lively green paint I ended up with was the natural choice. I had figured out a way to mesh their brand with mine, and the results were amazing.

The exclusivity, design challenges, and partnerships formed as a result of collaborations can take a brand to another level.

1. **HAVING SOMETHING TO SELL THAT *ONLY YOU HAVE ACCESS* TO ELEVATES YOUR BRAND.** Collaborations hand you something special that sets your brand apart from the competition. Market that for all it's worth... because it's worth a lot!

- -

2. **THE DESIGN CHALLENGES—*IF YOU CHOOSE TO TAKE THEM ON*—WILL ELEVATE YOUR CREATIVITY IN UNEXPECTED WAYS.** With Carrie's collaboration, I broke free from worrying about what others thought and designed from my heart. The Frances Valentine collab pushed me into a color scheme I had never dreamed of, and the results were mind-blowing.

- -

3. **HAVING YOUR OWN BUSINESS CAN BE ISOLATING.** Collaborations can give you new ideas and camaraderie, helping you see that you are not alone. When you can partner with other brands that complement your brand, you get to ride on each other's coattails. Being associated with another amazing brand elevates your brand in ways that you can't do alone.

CONCLUSION

Running a business takes a lot of common sense, and all these lessons I've learned over time. Scrutinizing a venue is key to reaching more customers—simply opening a shop doesn't mean customers will come to buy. You do not necessarily need an official degree to run your own business (*but you do need advisers*). Don't worry about impressing others with your business. Instead, make good decisions based on *your* bottom line. Having the courage to niche is key to standing out—otherwise you are just another boring fish in the large ocean. Want to make more money? You have to value your work, and price your goods or services higher than your comfort level. Know upfront that it takes a lot of time to build a brand because you are figuring it out along the way. Your business will become more meaningful if you find ways to use it to help others live better lives. It is up to you to make your own luck, don't just wish upon a star and expect things to happen. Pursue magazines for the credibility factor, but don't count on publicity making you money.

To get more done, focus on one thing at a time, and have one large umbrella goal for your business.

And finally, know the right collaborations can be key to moving your business forward.

Closing Thoughts

In my opinion, creativity is the single most important aspect to living a satisfying life. If nurtured and developed, creativity can permeate how we think, play, and work. We should never stop pursuing creativity—there is an infinite supply available to us if we will only just seek it out and practice.

Thinking more creatively is the beginning of this journey. Creative thinking begins with giving ourselves permission to dream. Then, by acknowledging the things that bring us joy, we welcome them into our lives. All these things are in our thoughts, and we have the power to gain control over those thoughts. Brainstorming is a part of my daily life. It helps me organize my ideas, see what is viable, and choose the best solutions. My hope is that my examples of taking risks have inspired and encouraged you to do the same. Our fears are just thoughts. Look your fears in the face, and do the hard thing anyway. The strategies in this book are only your beginning to creatively come up with new ideas and solve problems.

My sincere hope is that by seeing how I play, you will begin to plan ways to play that bring you joy. I know that I'm always inspired to play by seeing other people's homes and trying to incorporate more fun ideas into my own. That's why I wanted to share the spaces that inspire me, so that it will inspire you too. Now, you are ready to utilize some fun ways for mixing and matching fabrics, to style chairs, to upholster with a plan, and apply plenty of tips to approach your own chair makeovers. If you have troubling playing, then take time to do my "7-Day Play Everyday Challenge" in Chapter Six.

I can't believe I get to do chair styling and teaching for a living. While my enterprises still take effort and time, I still find it necessary to bring creativity into my work day. But as you read, remember I was on a long, hard journey to get where I am today. I trust you have discovered multiple ways to bring creativity into your jobs or businesses. If I make your pathway more direct with less hardship, that will bring me great joy.

Thank you for the honor of taking the time to read my book.

Let's keep in touch!

You can find me on all the social channels @chairwhimsy and on my website chairwhimsy.com.

I hope to hear from you!

Acknowledgments

First and foremost, I need to thank **Alexandra Styron.** Back in 2012, she bought my very first chair on Etsy. Without that order, none of this would have been possible.

I stand on the shoulders of my friends and mentors. They have been my support system throughout my journey. Judy and Grace are always willing to share margaritas and feedback to my crazy hare-brained ideas. Amy is one of my biggest fans and makes me great meals too! Thank you to my sweet neighbors who willingly dressed up and participated in my shenanigans down at the mansion. Julie Chenell, my super smart business coach who consistently gives me the best advice and told me to write this book! If it weren't for Tobi Fairly, my courses might never have existed... thank you for pushing me outside of my comfort zone. Selena Soo taught me the value of publicity and how to partner with others to improve my brand. My copywriter, Maci Wescott, who makes me sound much better than I actually do! Chase Kerlin, your mentorship has been invaluable to me. Vera Fischer, I'm so grateful for all the Starbucks meetings we had which guided me through my early challenges.

For the amazing individuals who helped me create the book I wanted to write... My book coach Nick Pavlidis, who had a wealth of knowledge that I could never have possessed, helped get my book off and running, and listened to my pathetic questions along the way. Without Debby Murphy, my words in this book would have fallen flat. Plus she's the best sounding board for all my crazy endeavors! Larissa Banting who's the best wordsmith and "hook"-er around. Abby Grace Photo used her mad photography skills to make me look better than I really do. Natalie McGuire is a designer like no other and used her powers to design my beautiful book as well as my website.

And finally, I want to thank my family. To my mom and my brother, some of my biggest fans, who allow me to brag—something you can only do with your family. My husband Blane, who really is a gem for putting up with my pink decorating obsession throughout our home—and for making me the best cocktails on the planet. I could never have been as supportive during the uncertain years, but I'm so grateful you were. And my girls, Raegan and Jordan. Everything I do, I do for you. Thanks for keeping me young at heart!

ACKNOWLEDGEMENTS

About the Author

Many people dream about making their passion project their career but few are able to turn their dreams into reality. Enter Wendy Conklin, who transformed her hobby into a powerhouse brand, Chair Whimsy, inspiring clients the world over to bring a sense of whimsy and joy into their living spaces.

Wendy was an educational consultant, busy writing books and helping teachers implement the latest in teaching techniques. While she enjoyed her job, she felt there was something missing from her career. She'd always had a creative streak but wasn't sure how to incorporate it into a lucrative business. In 2012, she took an upholstery course and was hooked. Styling her own chairs brought her an immense sense of satisfaction and a new decor dimension to her home. It wasn't long before friends began asking Wendy to help them "zhuzh" up their homes. Realizing she was onto something, she opened an Etsy store, offering custom refurbishing of antiques and flea-market finds.

Before long, Wendy found herself juggling her full-time job and the Etsy store, to the point something had to give. She realized that her misery as an employee was greater than the fear of becoming an entrepreneur. Springing into action, she took out a loan, asked for a six month leave of absence from work and set out to make her hobby a viable business. Within two days, she knew she could never return to her job and with the determination to make this new venture a success, she dug in.

Traction came quickly but in order to really make her new business soar, she knew she needed some outside advice and began working with a business coach. Contrary to popular belief that offering more options is the key to success, she niched down to a single focus - chairs. Wendy always had an artistic bend and by deciding to play by her own rules of fun, joy and lots of color, her **Chair Whimsy** brand caught flight, capturing the imaginations of clients around the world. In addition to her custom refurbished chairs, she expanded her line to include a collection of her unique designs made by artisans in Italy as well as fabric selection services.

In 2020, Wendy introduced her first course, *DIY Upholstery*, to teach others the joy of creating their own works of art. The response prompted her to create five more courses: *Styling with the Chair Stylist, Sourcing Swoon-Worthy Fabrics, Fabric Mixology, Just the Bottoms,* and *The Business of Chairs*. Dovetailing with the pandemic, the courses struck a nerve with thousands of women looking to learn a new skill while brightening up their homes. In under 18 months, sales for the courses hit over $500k. Encouraged by Wendy's enthusiasm and gentle instructions to play, create and not worry about somebody else's rules, these "Whimsies" are living the **Chair Whimsy** motto of "create the life you desire and a home that inspires you to live more creatively."

Wendy lives in Texas with her husband and furry friend, Maui, where she can be found puttering about in her handmade greenhouse; zipping about town in her floral Bug; or exploring the great outdoors in style with Willie, her revamped camper.

Discover more at:
ChairWhimsy.com